PROOF OF
LIFE ON EARTH

ALSO BY THE AUTHOR

- LAST RESORTS
- UNSCIENTIFIC AMERICANS
- PARALLEL UNIVERSES
- POEMS AND SONGS
- MONDO BOXO
- THE FOUR ELEMENTS

PROOF OF
LIFE ON EARTH

HarperPerennial
A Division of HarperCollins Publishers

FOR MY PARENTS

Of the 94 drawings in this collection, 80 originally appeared in The New Yorker. Copyright © 1988, 1989, 1990, 1991 by The New Yorker Magazine, Inc. Grateful acknowledgment is made to The New Yorker for permission to reprint.

Several cartoons have also appeared in The Sciences.

FIRST EDITION

LIBRARY OF CONGRESS CATALOGUE CARD NUMBER: 90-56417

ISBN: 0-06-096886-9

91 92 93 94 95 RRD 10 9 8 7 6 5 4 3 2 1

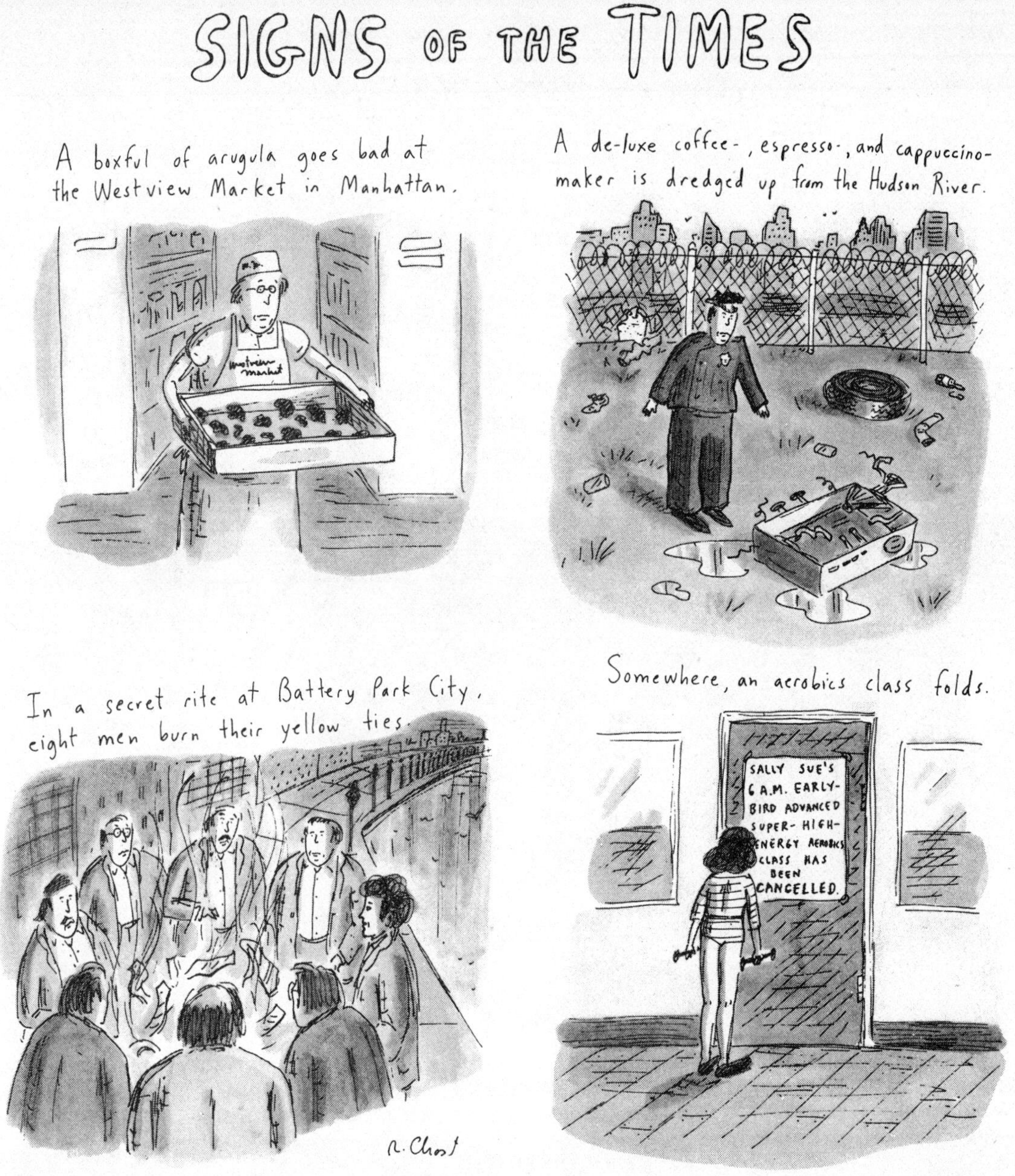
SIGNS OF THE TIMES
A boxful of arugula goes bad at the Westview Market in Manhattan.
A de-luxe coffee-, espresso-, and cappuccino-maker is dredged up from the Hudson River.
In a secret rite at Battery Park City, eight men burn their yellow ties.
Somewhere, an aerobics class folds.
SALLY SUE'S 6 A.M. EARLY-BIRD ADVANCED SUPER-HIGH-ENERGY AEROBICS CLASS HAS BEEN CANCELLED.
R. Chast

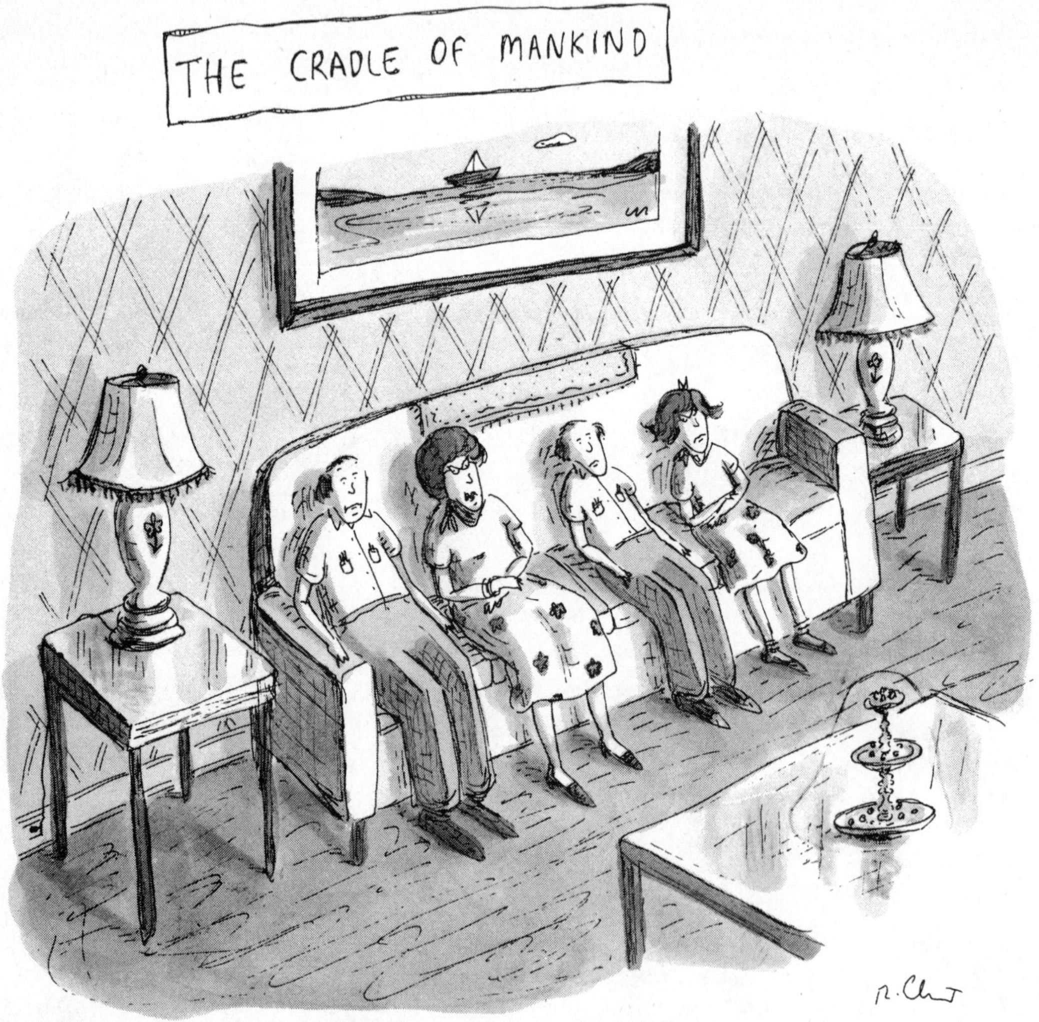
THE CRADLE OF MANKIND

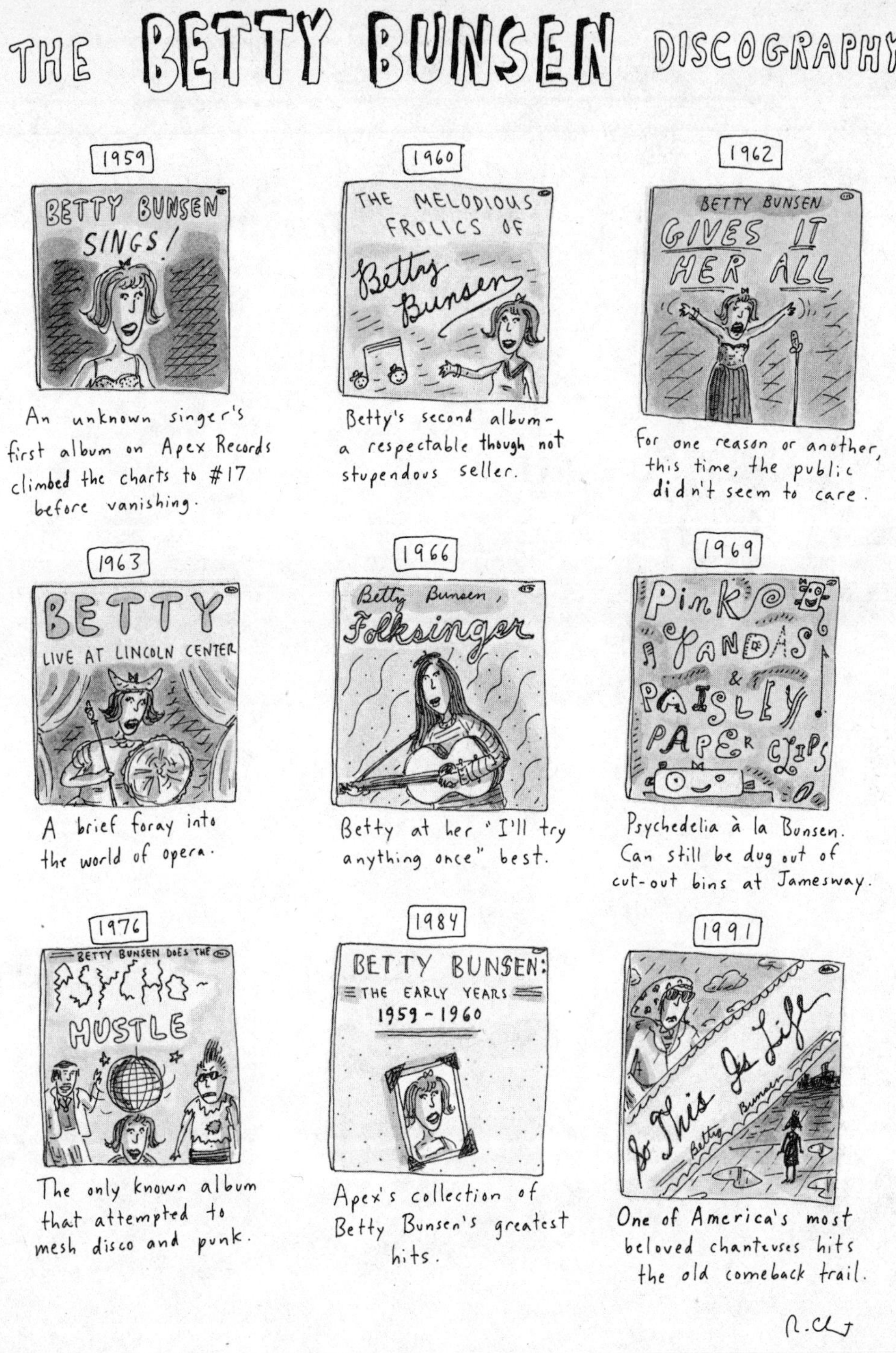
THE BETTY BUNSEN DISCOGRAPHY
1959
BETTY BUNSEN SINGS!
An unknown singer's first album on Apex Records climbed the charts to #17 before vanishing.
1960
THE MELODIOUS FROLICS OF Betty Bunsen
Betty's second album - a respectable though not stupendous seller.
1962
BETTY BUNSEN GIVES IT HER ALL
For one reason or another, this time, the public didn't seem to care.
1963
BETTY LIVE AT LINCOLN CENTER
A brief foray into the world of opera.
1966
Betty Bunsen, Folksinger
Betty at her "I'll try anything once" best.
1969
Pink Pandas & Paisley Paper Clips
Psychedelia à la Bunsen. Can still be dug out of cut-out bins at Jamesway.
1976
BETTY BUNSEN DOES THE PSYCHO-HUSTLE
The only known album that attempted to mesh disco and punk.
1984
BETTY BUNSEN: THE EARLY YEARS 1959-1960
Apex's collection of Betty Bunsen's greatest hits.
1991
So This Is Life
Betty Bunsen
One of America's most beloved chanteuses hits the old comeback trail.
R. Chast

Why One's Parents Got Married

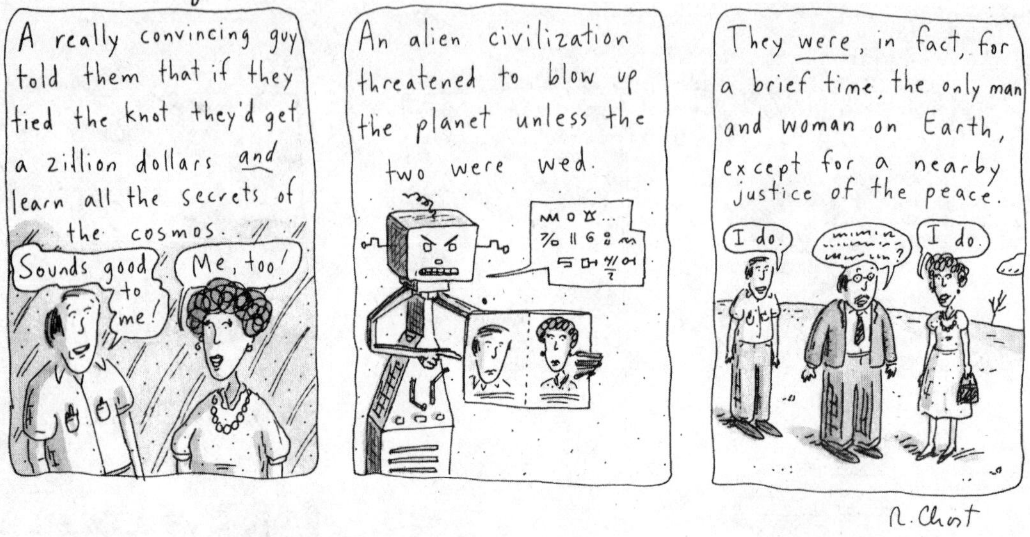

A really convincing guy told them that if they tied the knot they'd get a zillion dollars and learn all the secrets of the cosmos.
Sounds good to me!
Me, too!
An alien civilization threatened to blow up the planet unless the two were wed.
They were, in fact, for a brief time, the only man and woman on Earth, except for a nearby justice of the peace.
I do.
I do.
R. Chast

The Very Last Dinosaur

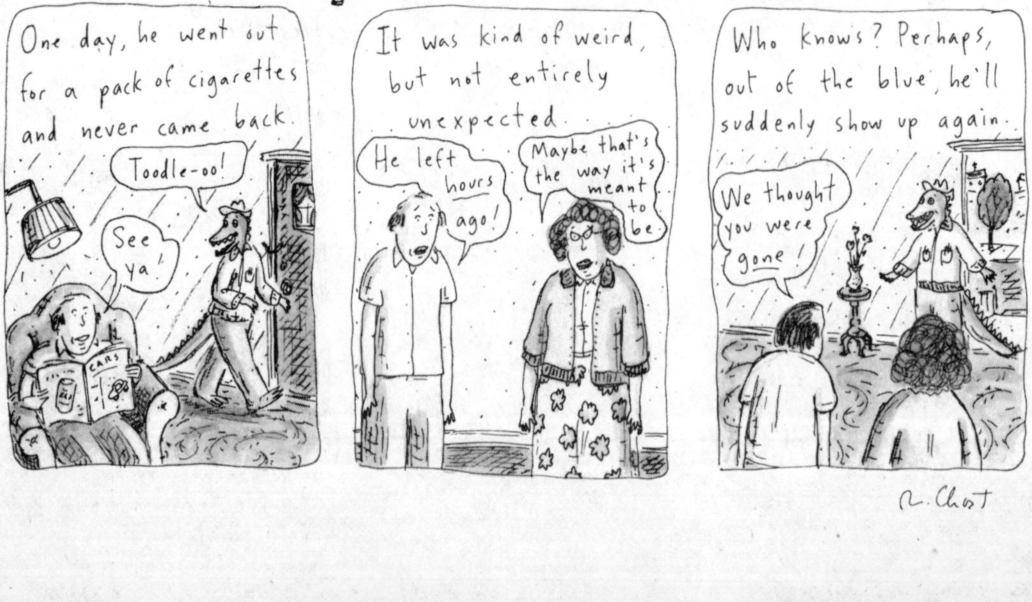

One day, he went out for a pack of cigarettes and never came back.
Toodle-oo!
See ya!
CARS
It was kind of weird, but not entirely unexpected.
He left hours ago!
Maybe that's the way it's meant to be.
Who knows? Perhaps, out of the blue, he'll suddenly show up again.
We thought you were gone!
R. Chast

ED GOES GREEN

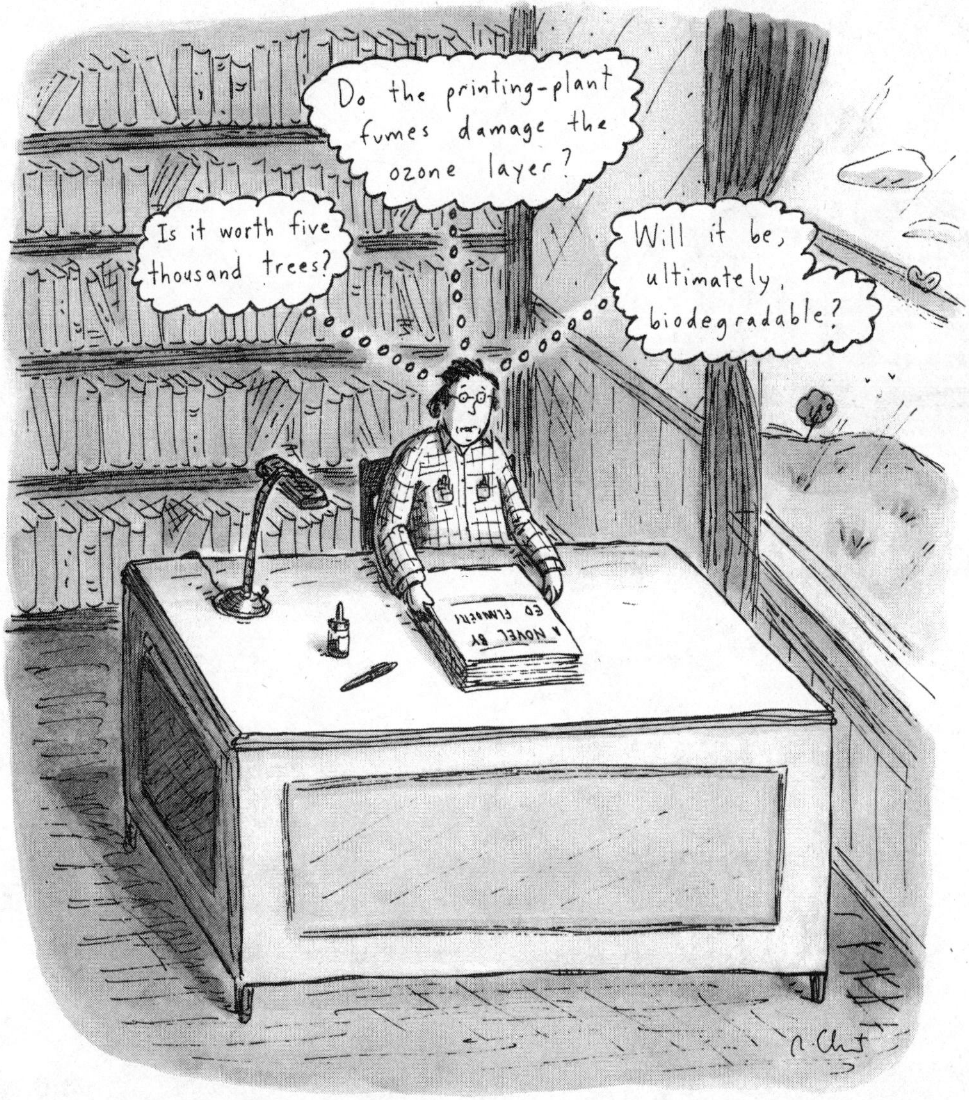
Is it worth five thousand trees?
Do the printing-plant fumes damage the ozone layer?
Will it be, ultimately, biodegradable?

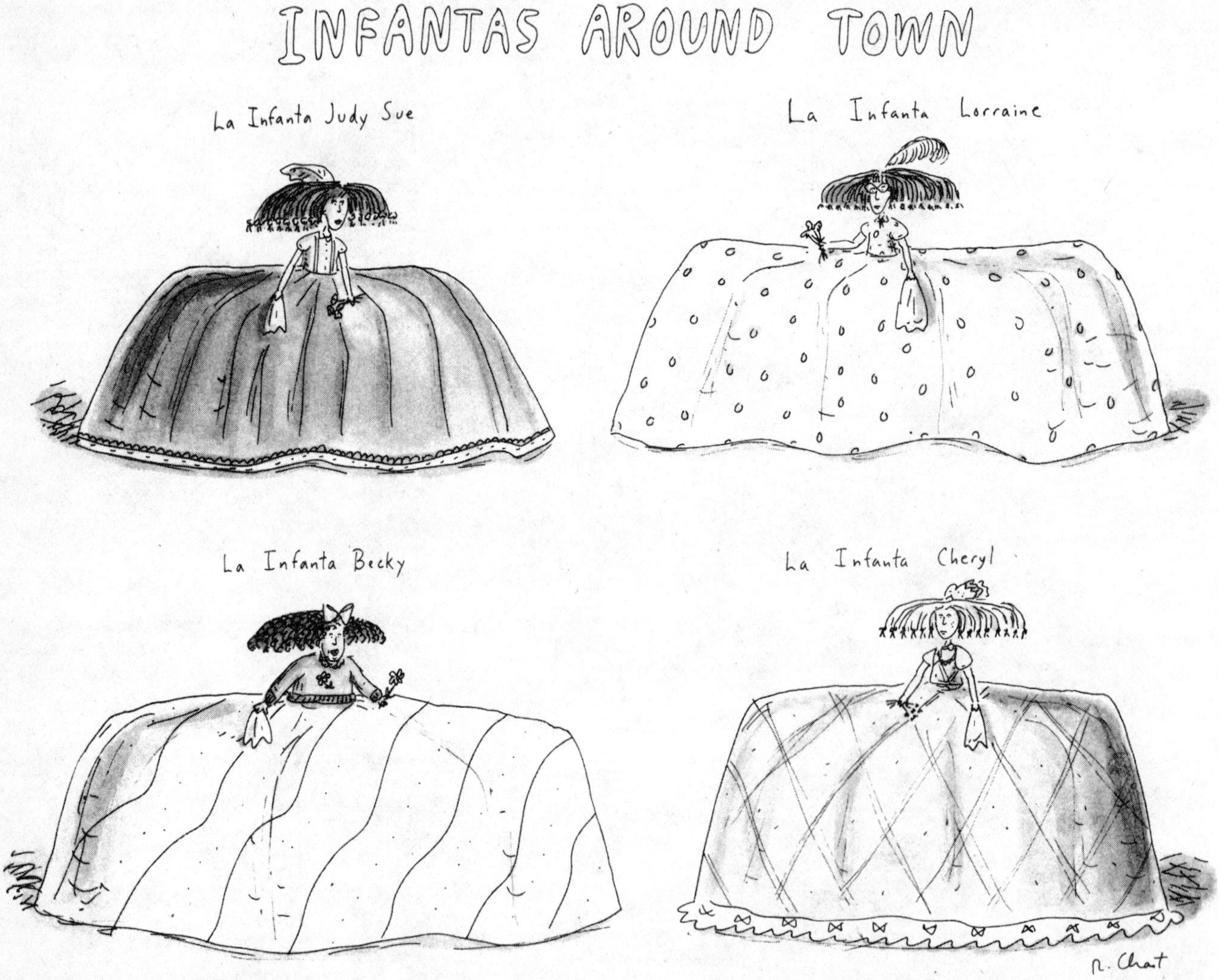
INFANTAS AROUND TOWN
La Infanta Judy Sue
La Infanta Lorraine
La Infanta Becky
La Infanta Cheryl
R. Chast

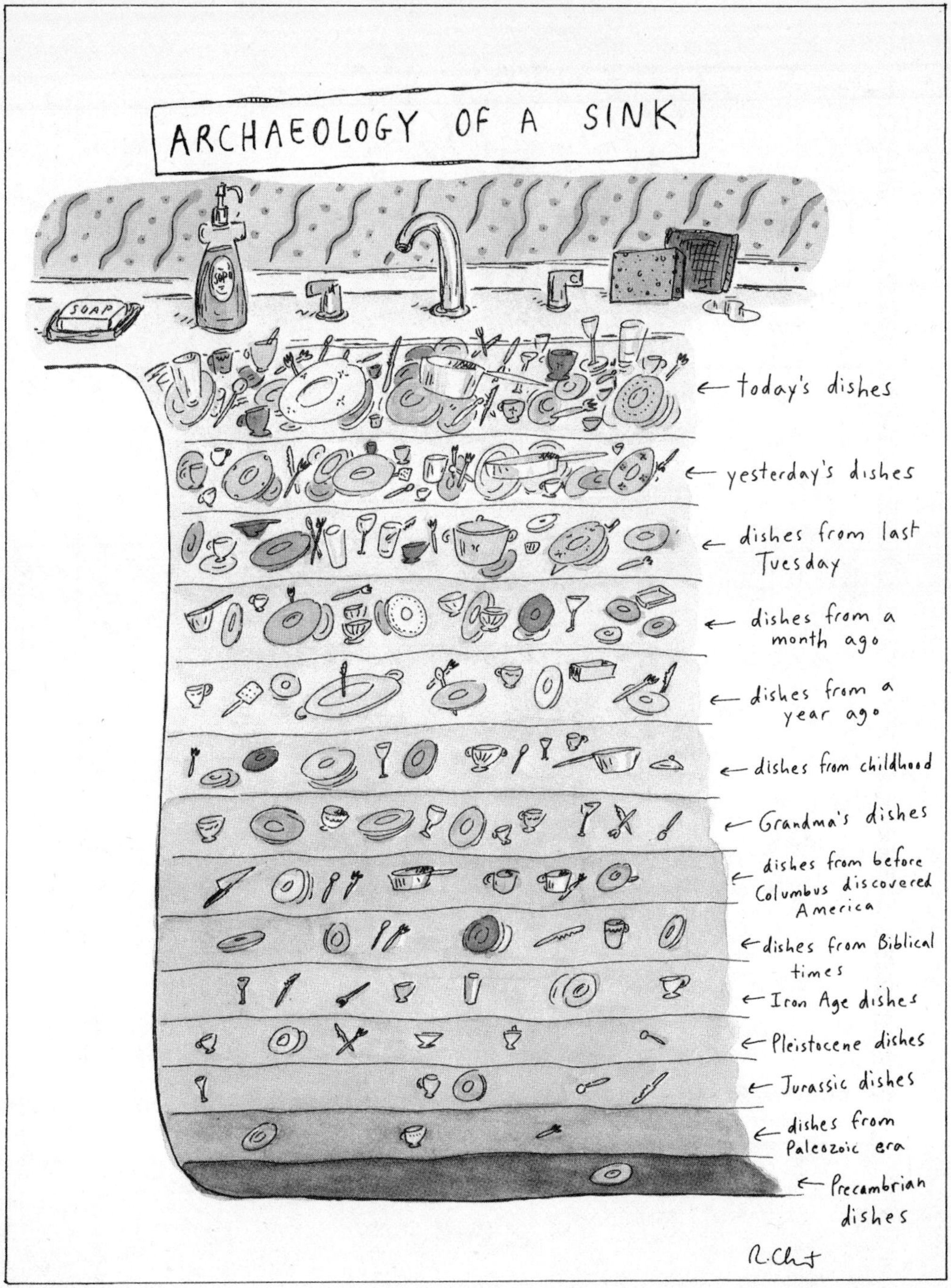
ARCHAEOLOGY OF A SINK
SOAP
← today's dishes
← yesterday's dishes
← dishes from last Tuesday
← dishes from a month ago
← dishes from a year ago
← dishes from childhood
← Grandma's dishes
← dishes from before Columbus discovered America
← dishes from Biblical times
← Iron Age dishes
← Pleistocene dishes
← Jurassic dishes
← dishes from Paleozoic era
← Precambrian dishes
R. Chast

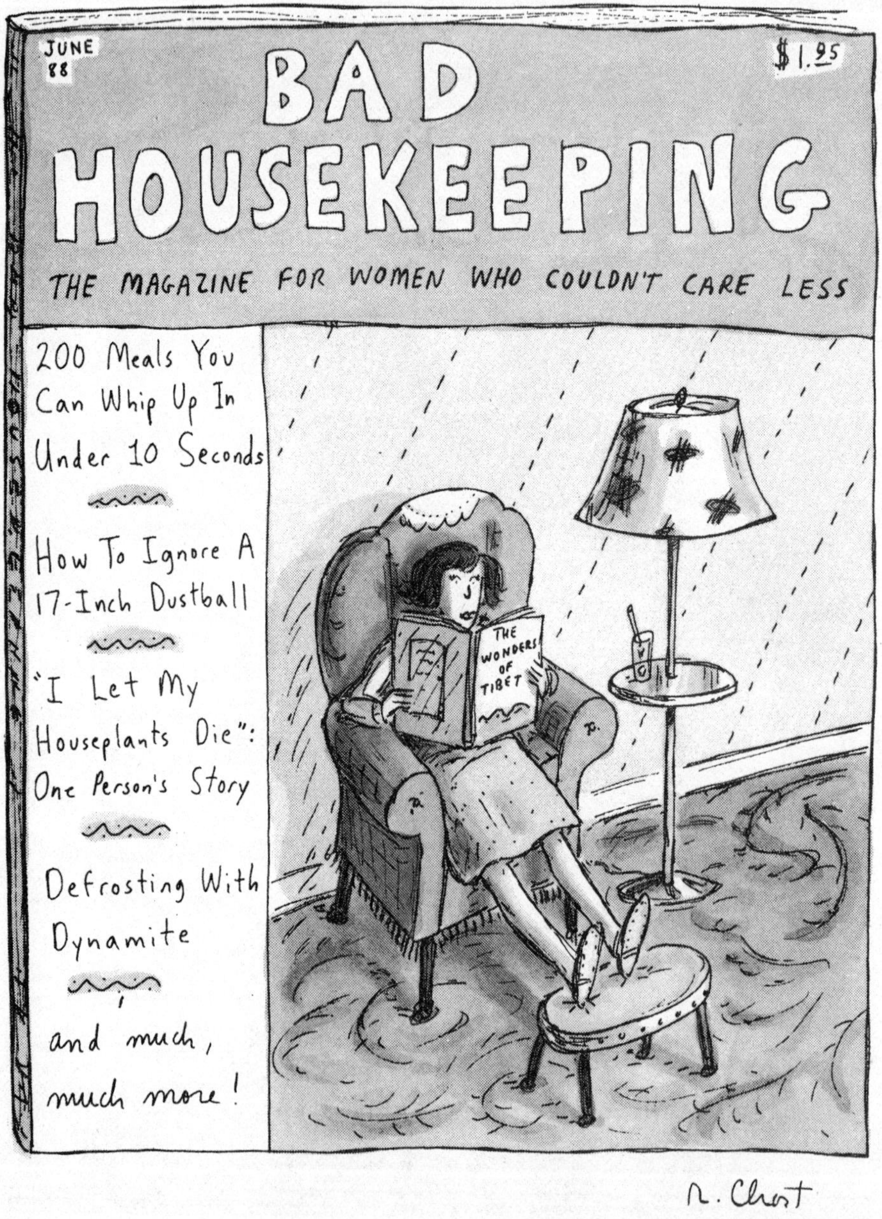
JUNE 88
$1.95
BAD HOUSEKEEPING
THE MAGAZINE FOR WOMEN WHO COULDN'T CARE LESS
200 Meals You Can Whip Up In Under 10 Seconds
How To Ignore A 17-Inch Dustball
"I Let My Houseplants Die": One Person's Story
Defrosting With Dynamite
and much, much more!
THE WONDERS OF TIBET
R. Chast

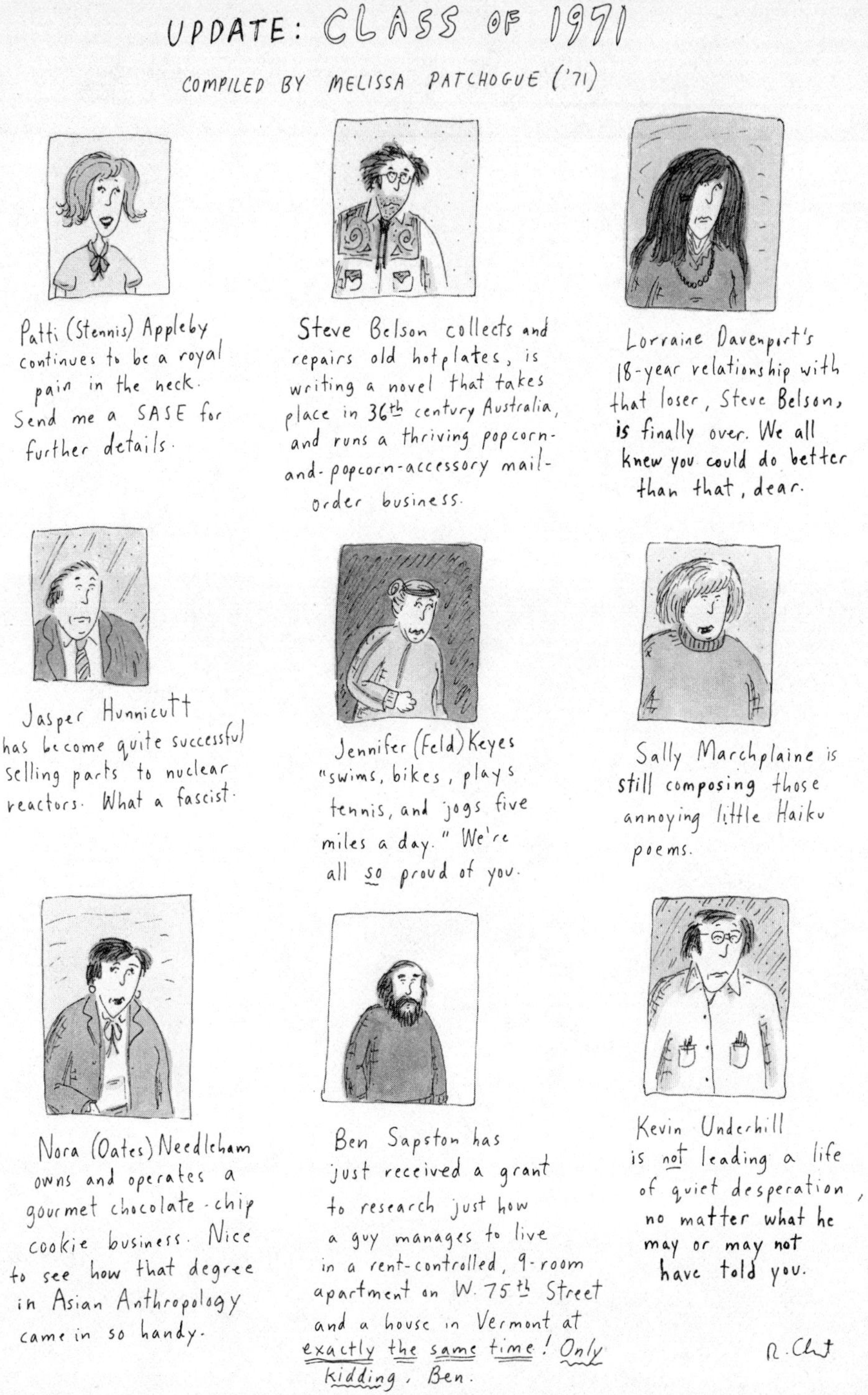
UPDATE: CLASS OF 1971
COMPILED BY MELISSA PATCHOGUE ('71)
Patti (Stennis) Appleby continues to be a royal pain in the neck. Send me a SASE for further details.
Steve Belson collects and repairs old hotplates, is writing a novel that takes place in 36th century Australia, and runs a thriving popcorn-and-popcorn-accessory mail-order business.
Lorraine Davenport's 18-year relationship with that loser, Steve Belson, is finally over. We all knew you could do better than that, dear.
Jasper Hunnicutt has become quite successful selling parts to nuclear reactors. What a fascist.
Jennifer (Feld) Keyes "swims, bikes, plays tennis, and jogs five miles a day." We're all so proud of you.
Sally Marchplaine is still composing those annoying little Haiku poems.
Nora (Oates) Needleham owns and operates a gourmet chocolate-chip cookie business. Nice to see how that degree in Asian Anthropology came in so handy.
Ben Sapston has just received a grant to research just how a guy manages to live in a rent-controlled, 9-room apartment on W. 75th Street and a house in Vermont at exactly the same time! Only kidding, Ben.
Kevin Underhill is not leading a life of quiet desperation, no matter what he may or may not have told you.
R. Chast

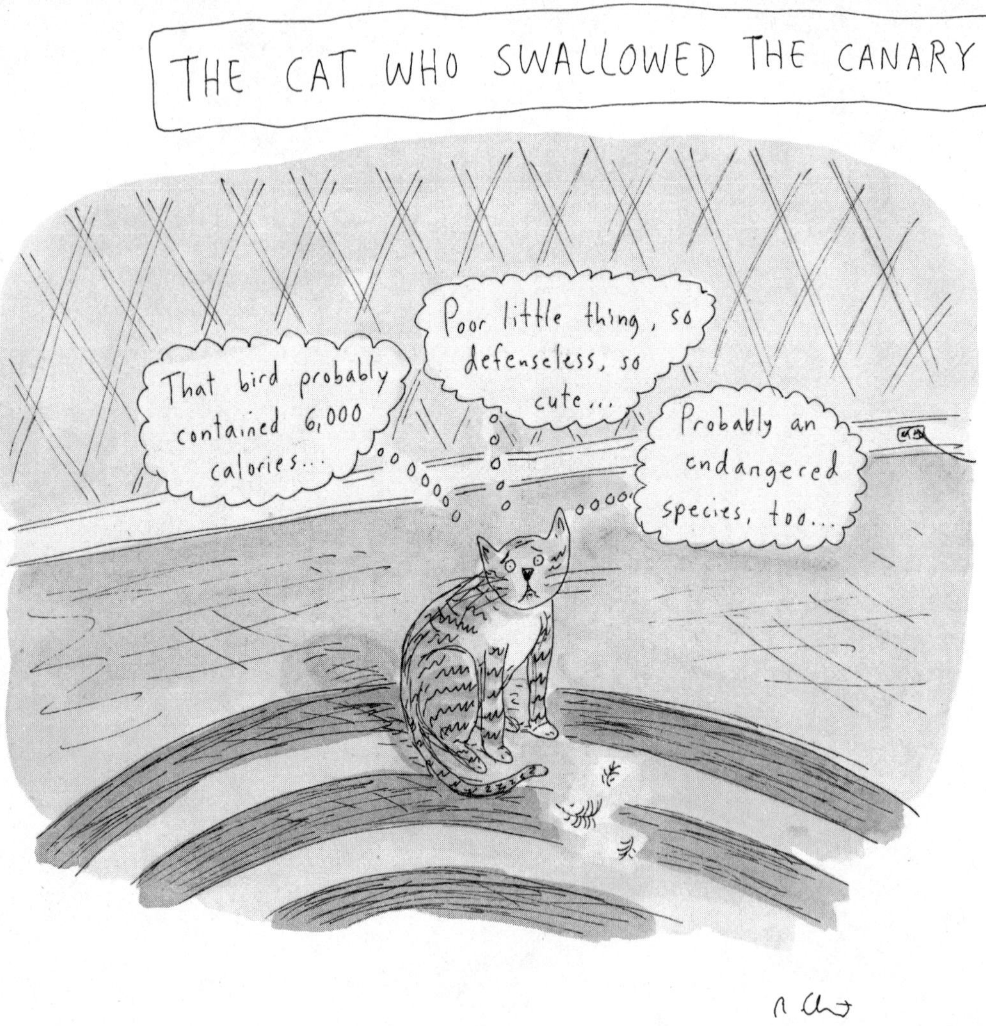
THE CAT WHO SWALLOWED THE CANARY
That bird probably contained 6,000 calories...
Poor little thing, so defenseless, so cute...
Probably an endangered species, too...

FUSSBUDGET 1989

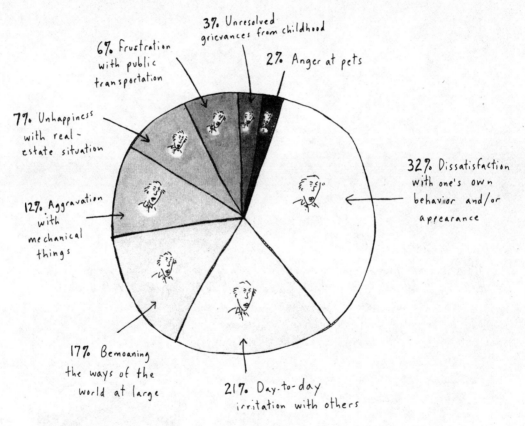

3% Unresolved grievances from childhood

6% Frustration with public transportation

2% Anger at pets

7% Unhappiness with real-estate situation

32% Dissatisfaction with one's own behavior and/or appearance

12% Aggravation with mechanical things

17% Bemoaning the ways of the world at large

21% Day-to-day irritation with others

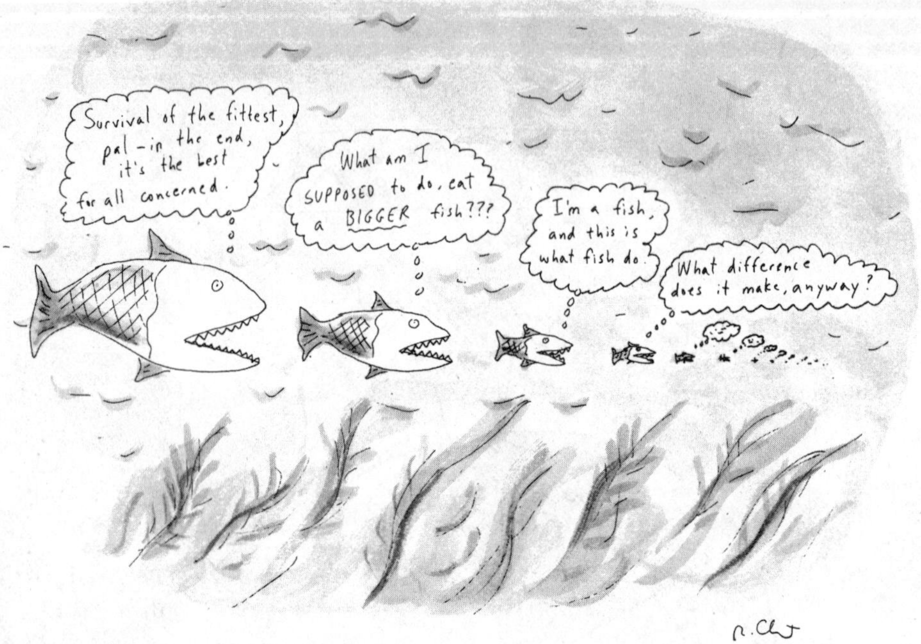
Survival of the fittest, pal – in the end, it's the best for all concerned.
What am I SUPPOSED to do, eat a BIGGER fish???
I'm a fish, and this is what fish do.
What difference does it make, anyway?
R. Chast

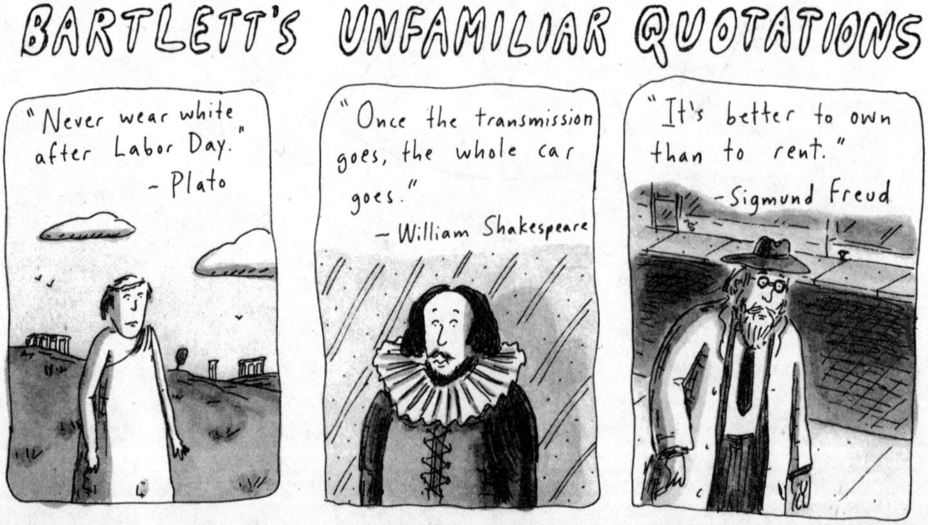
BARTLETT'S UNFAMILIAR QUOTATIONS
"Never wear white after Labor Day." – Plato
"Once the transmission goes, the whole car goes." – William Shakespeare
"It's better to own than to rent." – Sigmund Freud
R. Chast

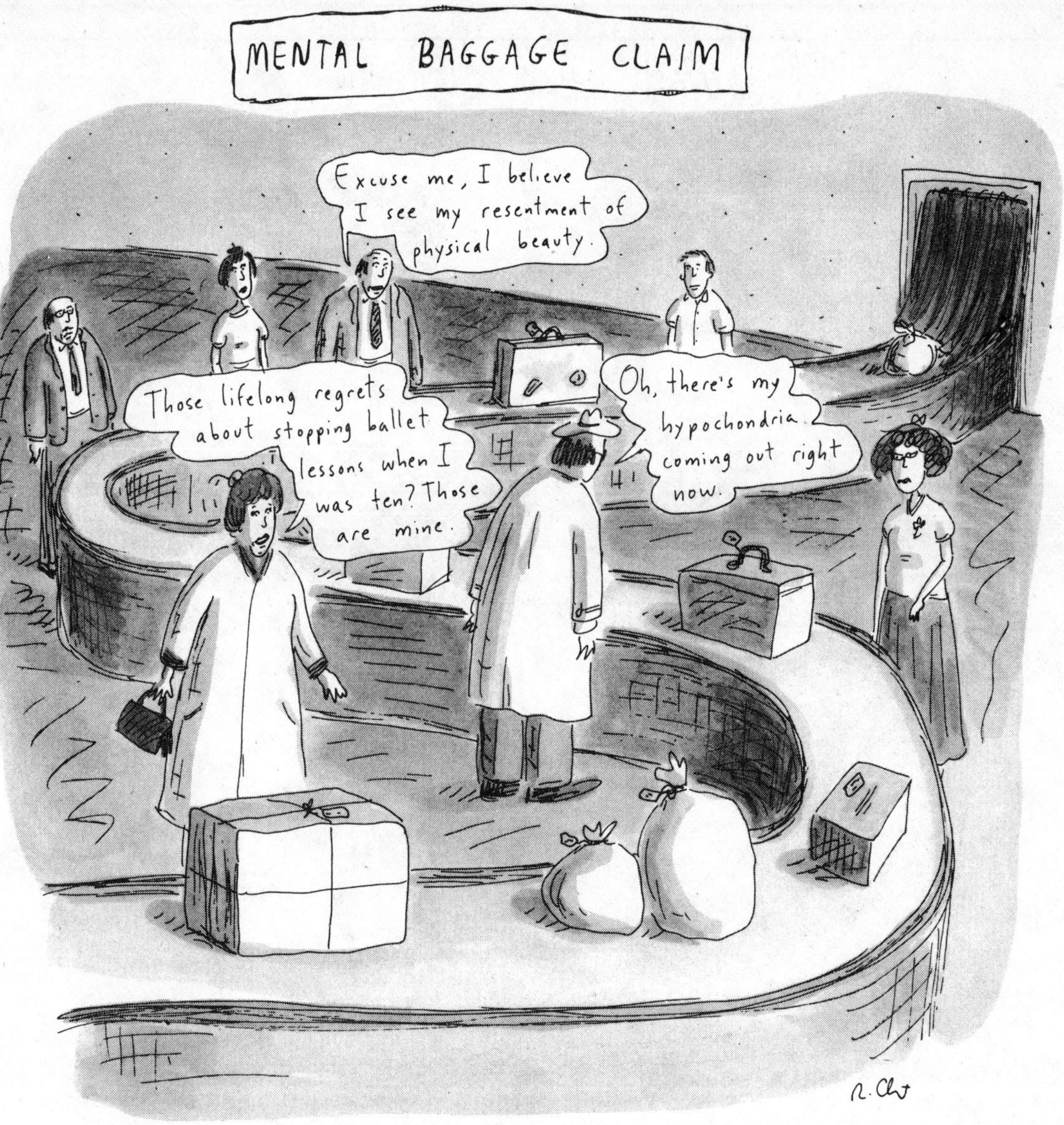
MENTAL BAGGAGE CLAIM
Excuse me, I believe I see my resentment of physical beauty.
Those lifelong regrets about stopping ballet lessons when I was ten? Those are mine.
Oh, there's my hypochondria coming out right now.

KWALITY TIME

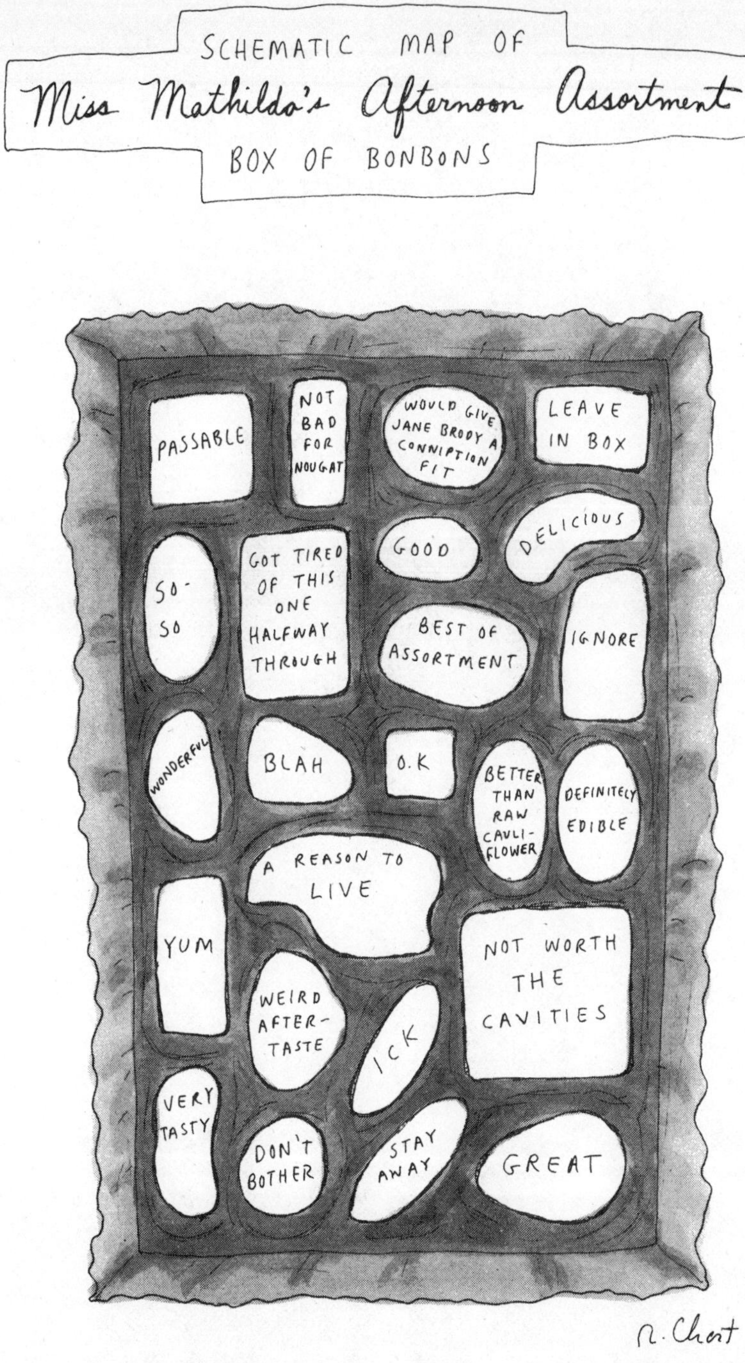
SCHEMATIC MAP OF
Miss Mathilda's Afternoon Assortment
BOX OF BONBONS
PASSABLE
NOT BAD FOR NOUGAT
WOULD GIVE JANE BRODY A CONNIPTION FIT
LEAVE IN BOX
GOOD
DELICIOUS
SO-SO
GOT TIRED OF THIS ONE HALFWAY THROUGH
BEST OF ASSORTMENT
IGNORE
WONDERFUL
BLAH
O.K
BETTER THAN RAW CAULI-FLOWER
DEFINITELY EDIBLE
A REASON TO LIVE
YUM
NOT WORTH THE CAVITIES
WEIRD AFTER-TASTE
ICK
VERY TASTY
DON'T BOTHER
STAY AWAY
GREAT
R. Chast

DOGGEREL IN MOTION

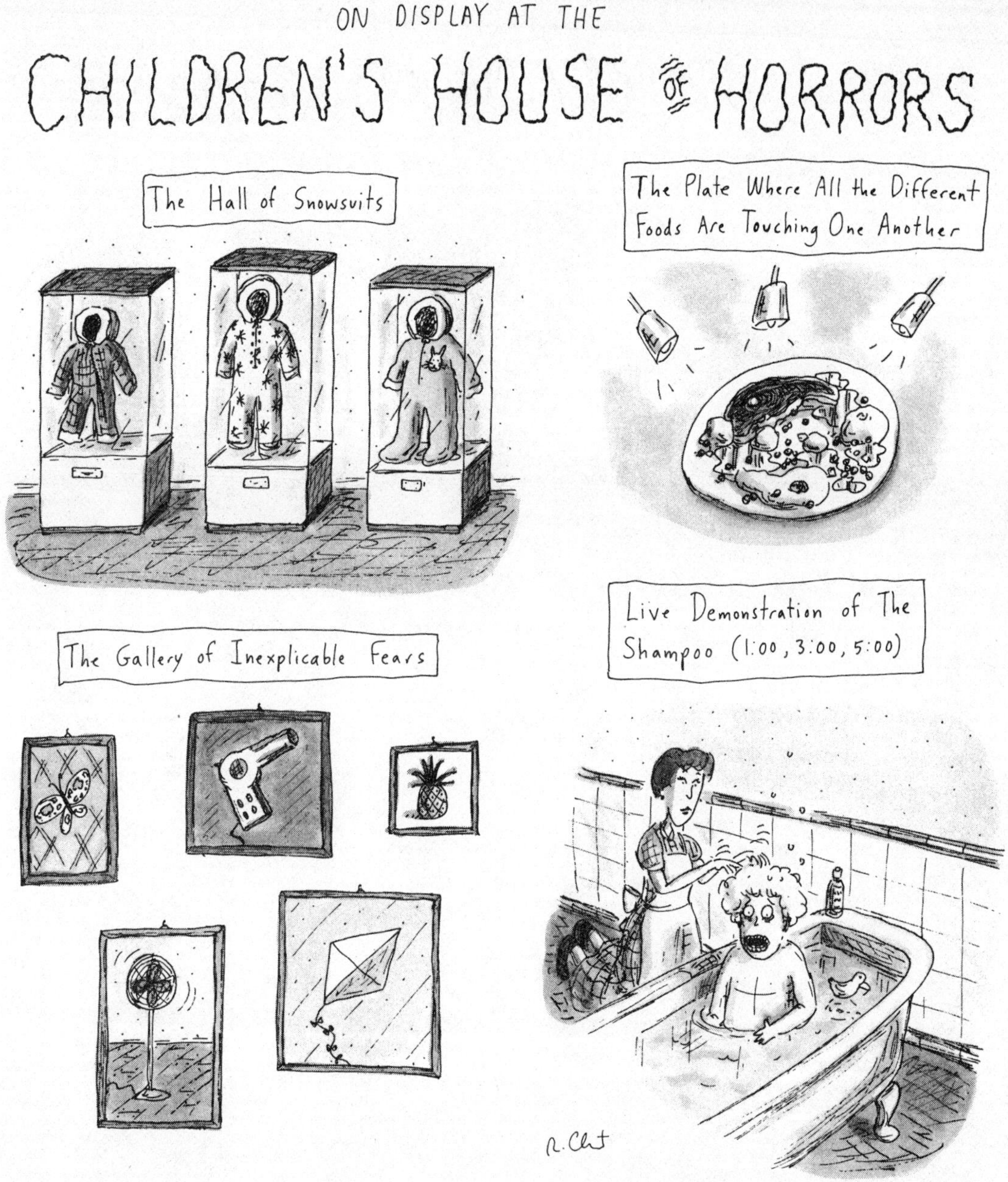
ON DISPLAY AT THE
CHILDREN'S HOUSE OF HORRORS
The Hall of Snowsuits
The Plate Where All the Different Foods Are Touching One Another
The Gallery of Inexplicable Fears
Live Demonstration of The Shampoo (1:00, 3:00, 5:00)

The SPONTANEOUS GOURMET

"Sometimes something happens ... and sometimes it doesn't."

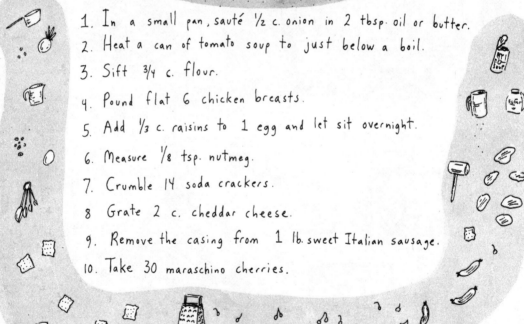

1. In a small pan, sauté ½ c. onion in 2 tbsp. oil or butter.
2. Heat a can of tomato soup to just below a boil.
3. Sift ¾ c. flour.
4. Pound flat 6 chicken breasts.
5. Add ⅓ c. raisins to 1 egg and let sit overnight.
6. Measure ⅛ tsp. nutmeg.
7. Crumble 14 soda crackers.
8. Grate 2 c. cheddar cheese.
9. Remove the casing from 1 lb. sweet Italian sausage.
10. Take 30 maraschino cherries.

R. Chast

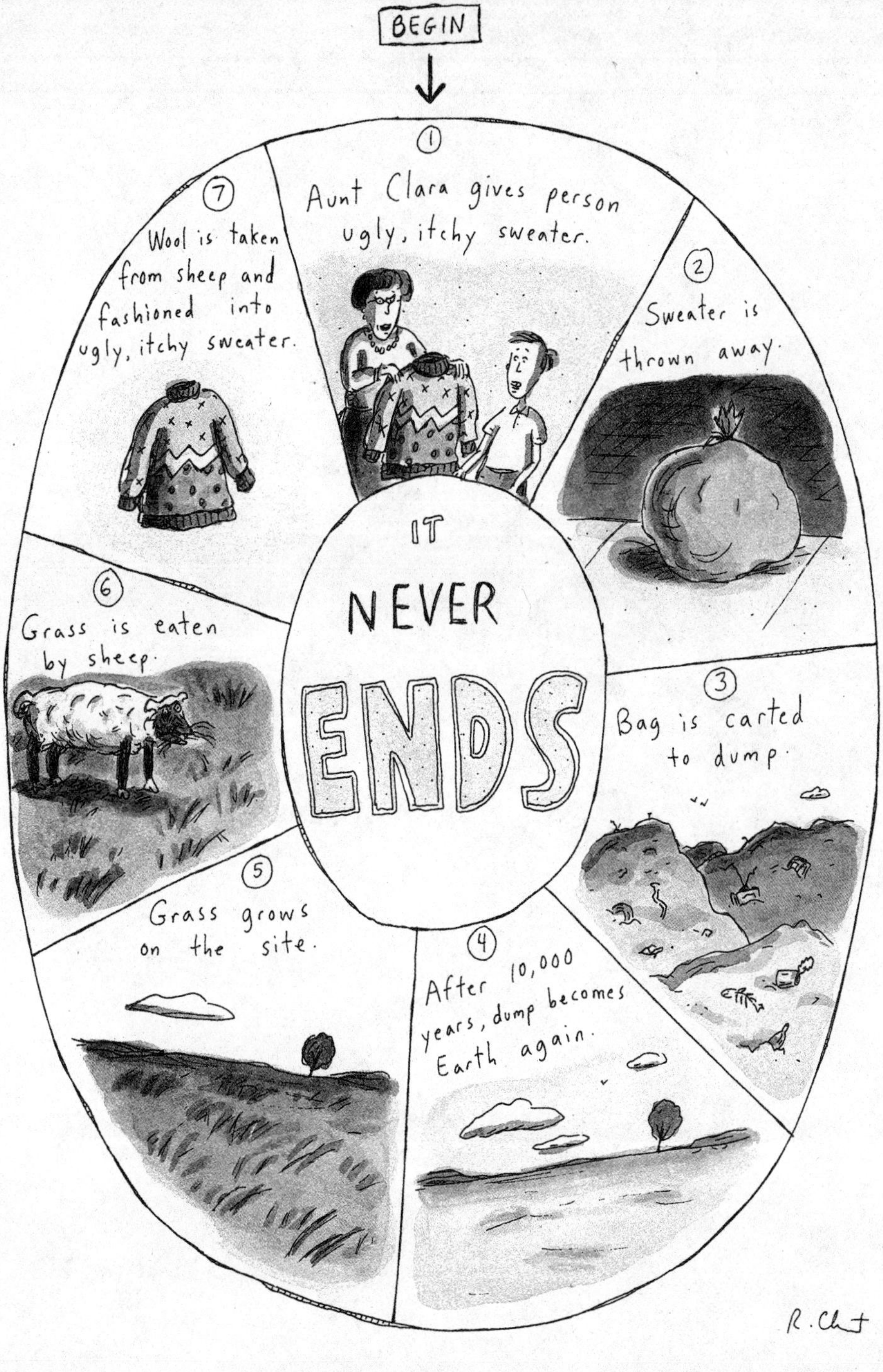
BEGIN
IT NEVER ENDS
1
Aunt Clara gives person ugly, itchy sweater.
2
Sweater is thrown away.
3
Bag is carted to dump.
4
After 10,000 years, dump becomes Earth again.
5
Grass grows on the site.
6
Grass is eaten by sheep.
7
Wool is taken from sheep and fashioned into ugly, itchy sweater.
R. Chast

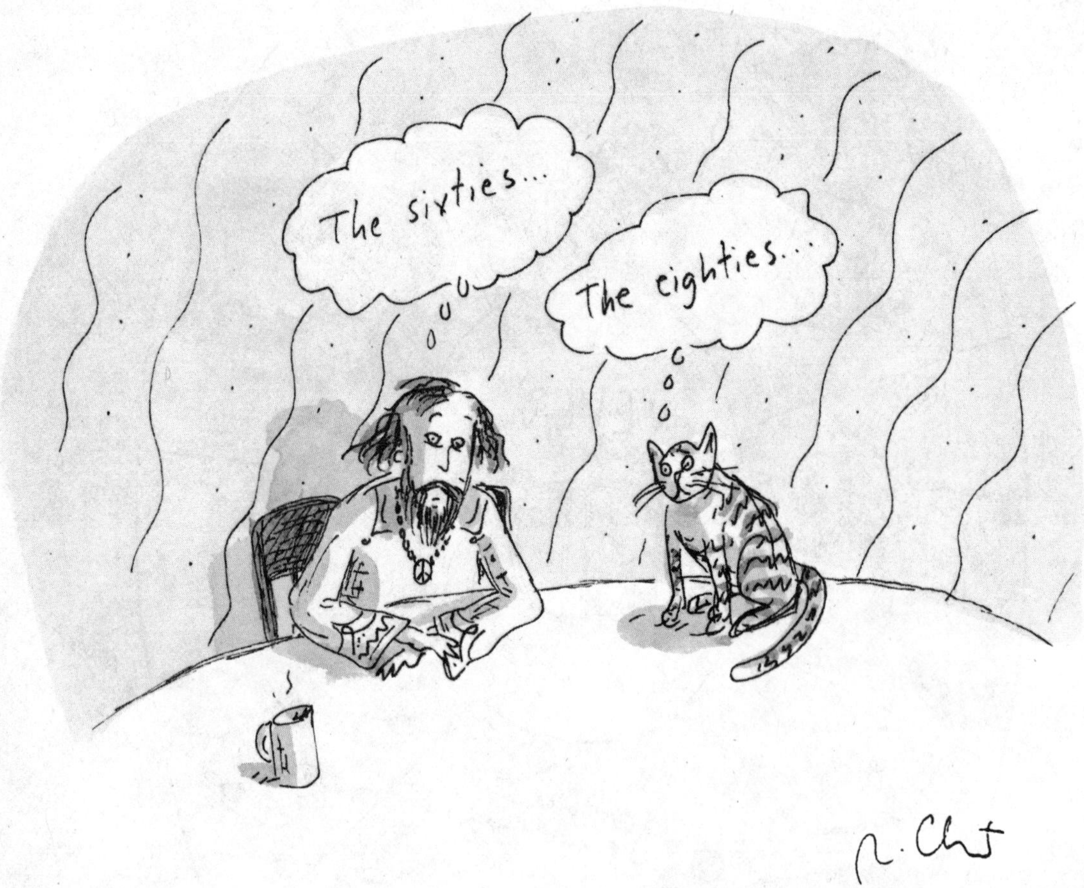
The sixties...
The eighties...
R. Chast

TRAVELOGUE

Somewhere out there is a planet where everything is extremely clean.

If a speck of dust falls from the sky, ten people fight each other over who gets to pick it up.

I saw it first!

You are such a LIAR!!!

An inhabitant would no sooner leave a piece of old macaroni on the kitchen floor—

Aaaagh- I'll get it next time something falls.

—than slap someone in the face for no reason at all.

OW! Whydja do that??

There are 70,000 words for "clean" on this planet.

spenky   pidgco   dr
blerk   fastebine biss
nt   cludge   spa
ssit   foonio   leb
         cobcaw   ze

National heroes and heroines have more to do with cleanliness than bravery or intelligence.

TILLIE KRAUS: YOU COULD EAT OFF HER FLOORS

And the jails are chock full of people who made cookies and then didn't clean up the mess.

I was going to do it later!

Of course, there are a few rebels.

Let's go out and spill some stuff!

YEAH!!!

NEXT WEEK: A VISIT TO *THE QUIET PLANET*

Sh-h-h!

r. Chst

If you're interested in entering the high-paying world of TV journalism, first you must learn

THE ART OF BANTERING!

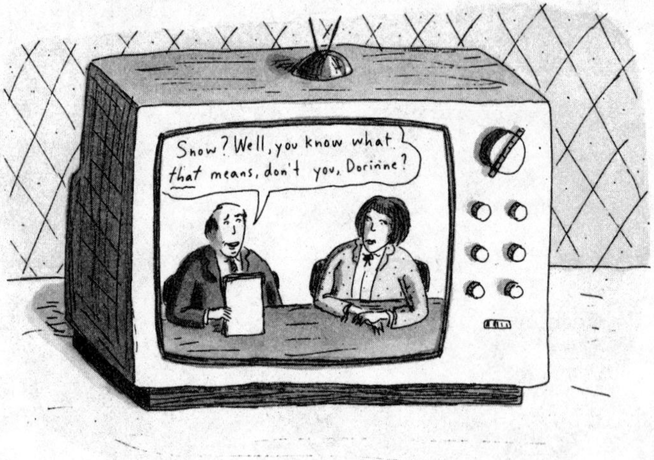
Snow? Well, you know what *that* means, don't you, Dorinne?

You'll learn about:

- The ever-popular weather banter
- News bantering: which topics are good, which topics are maybe not so good
- Holiday bantering
- What to do when you hit a "banter wall": EMERGENCY BANTER
- Free-form bantering (for the advanced)

SIMPLY CHECK ONE:

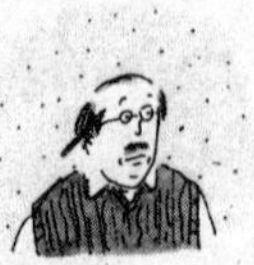

☐ Yes, please send me my Banter Info-Pak

☐ No, I'd rather not know one tiny thing more about this topic

R. Chast

CASH MACHINES from ACROSS THE LAND

The Big Purse
East Lubbock, New Jersey.

Dad's Pocket Casheteria
Twelve Buckets, Nebraska

The Weeping Bankbook
Hensteeth, Alabama

Mattress o' Moola
Knorl, Idaho

R.Chast

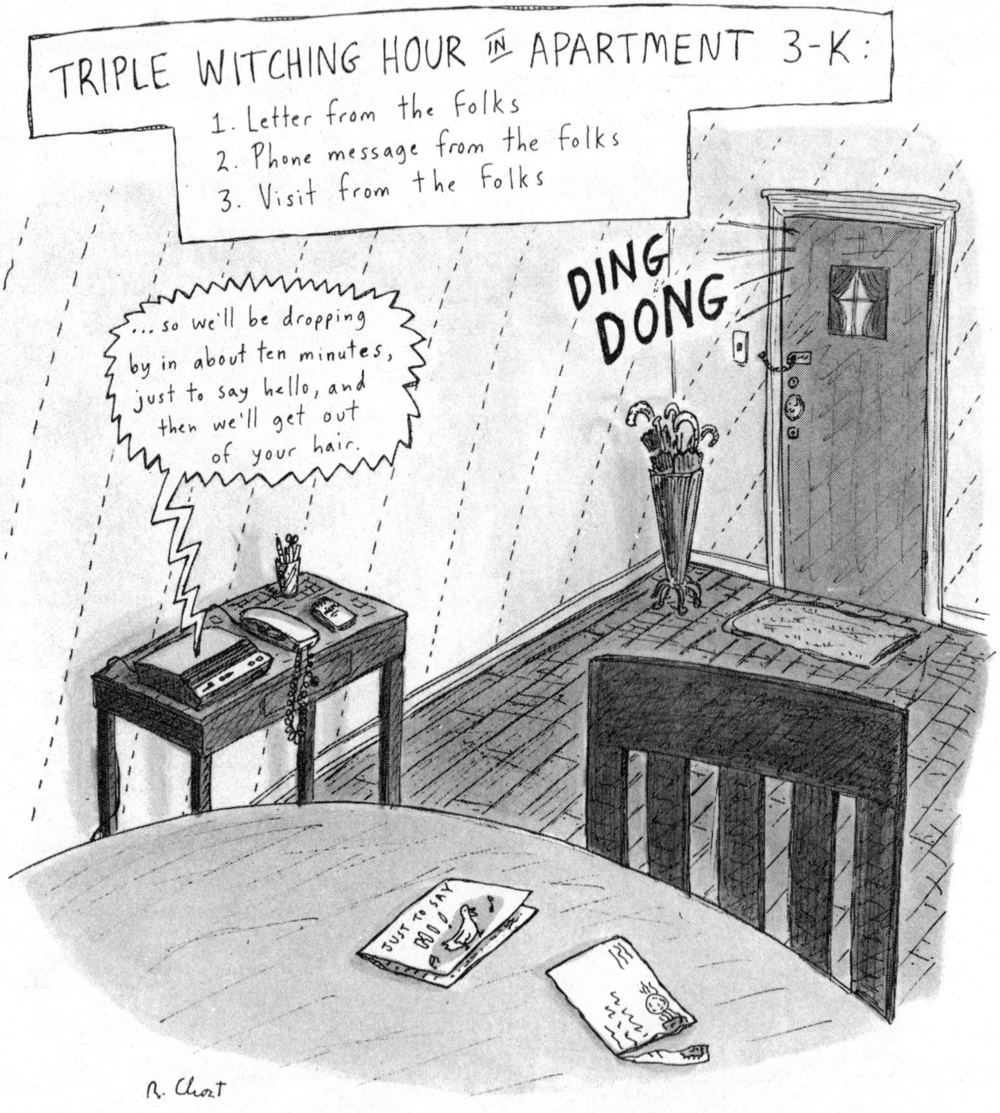
TRIPLE WITCHING HOUR IN APARTMENT 3-K:
1. Letter from the Folks
2. Phone message from the folks
3. Visit from the Folks
...so we'll be dropping by in about ten minutes, just to say hello, and then we'll get out of your hair.
DING DONG
JUST TO SAY
R. Chast

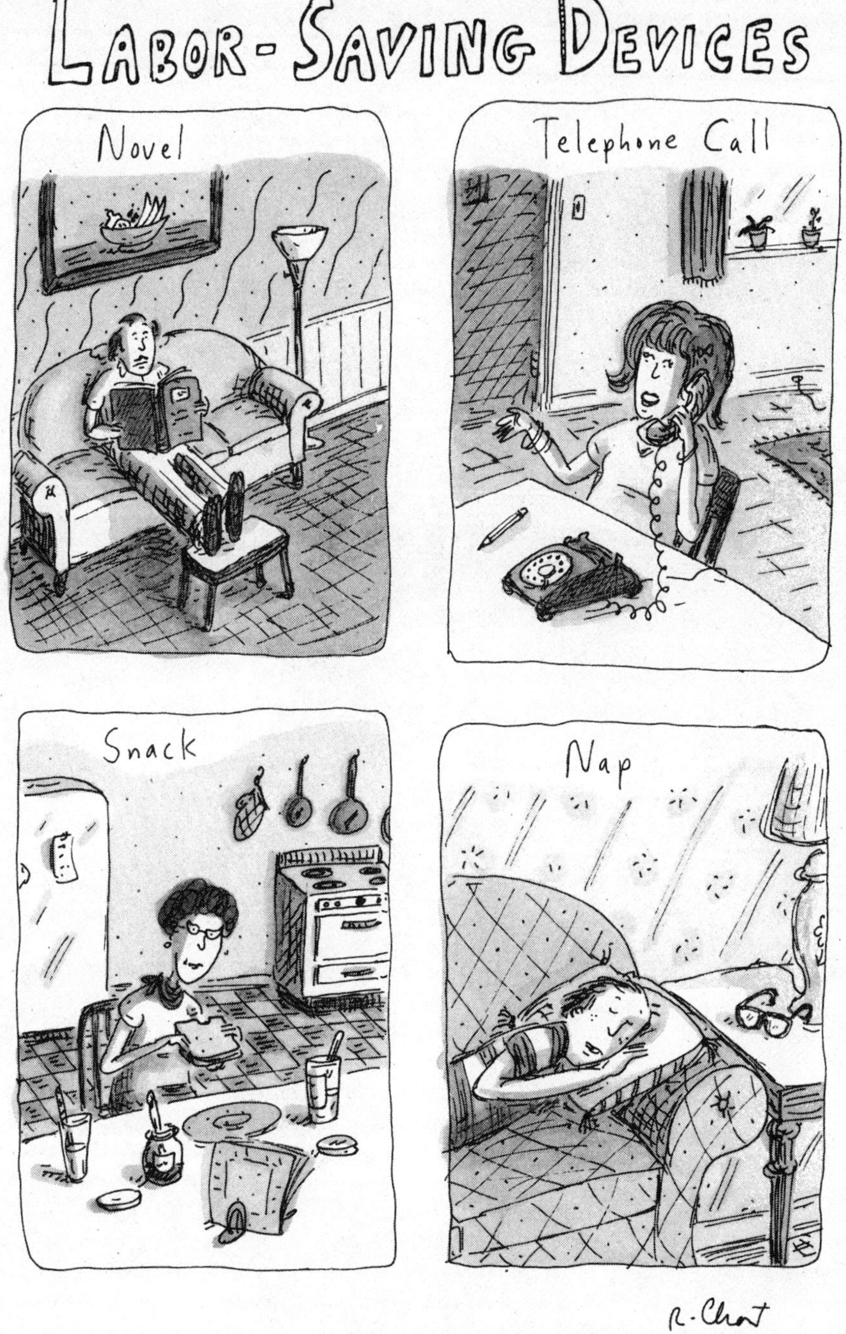
LABOR-SAVING DEVICES
Novel
Telephone Call
Snack
Nap
R. Chast

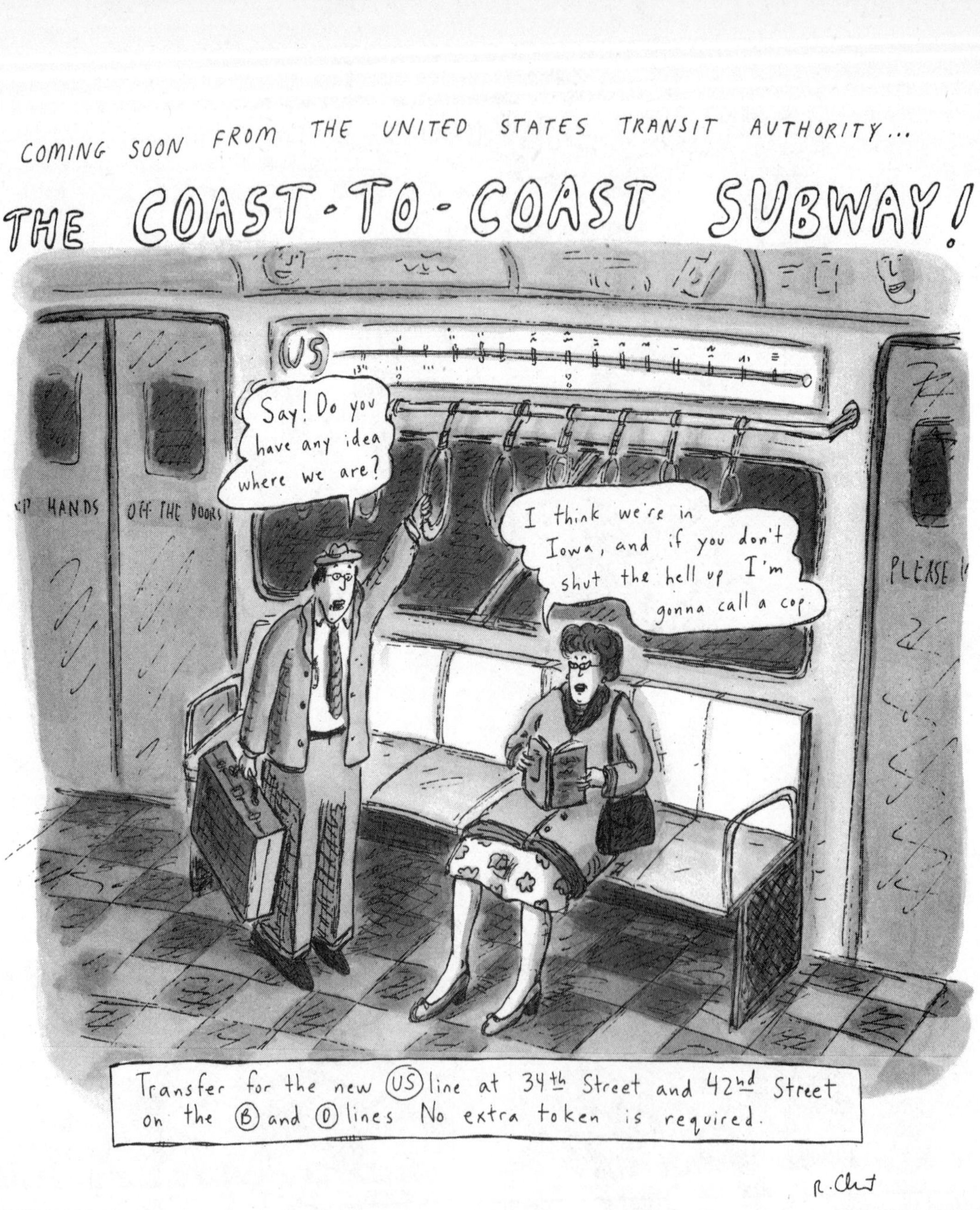
COMING SOON FROM THE UNITED STATES TRANSIT AUTHORITY...
THE COAST-TO-COAST SUBWAY!
Say! Do you have any idea where we are?
I think we're in Iowa, and if you don't shut the hell up I'm gonna call a cop.
Transfer for the new US line at 34th Street and 42nd Street on the B and D lines. No extra token is required.
R. Chast

Special Features of Apartment 10-L

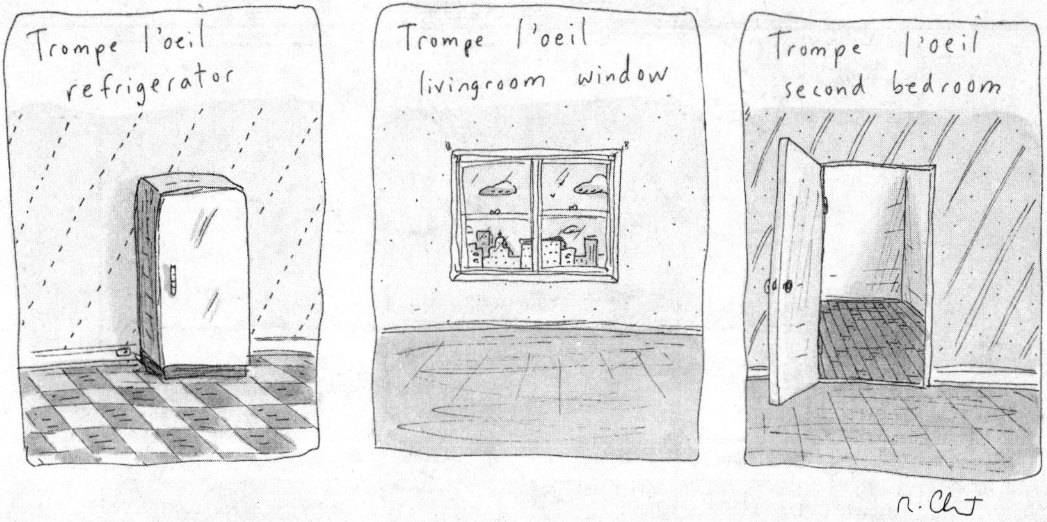
Trompe l'oeil refrigerator
Trompe l'oeil livingroom window
Trompe l'oeil second bedroom

SURPRISINGLY AFFORDABLE

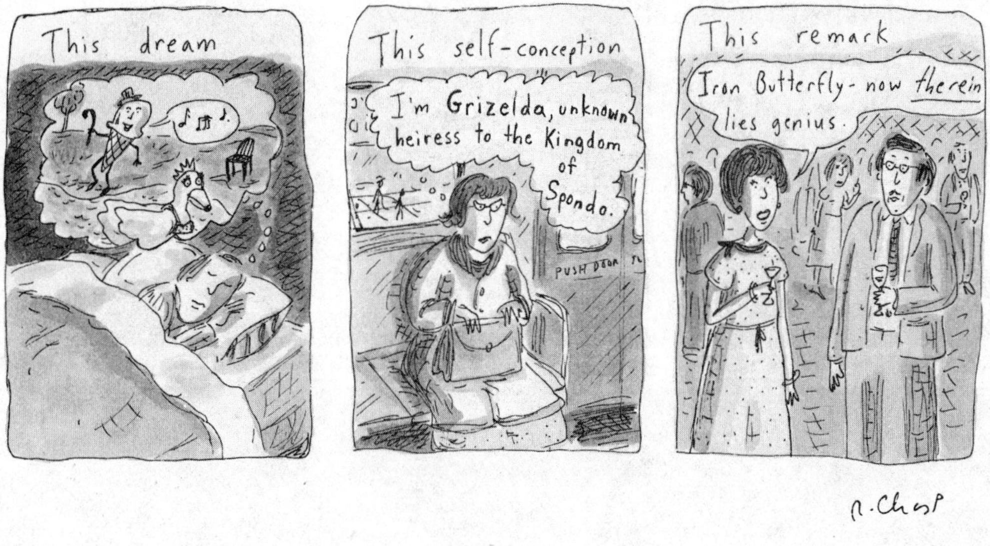
This dream
This self-conception
I'm Grizelda, unknown heiress to the Kingdom of Spondo.
PUSH DOOR
This remark
Iron Butterfly - now therein lies genius.

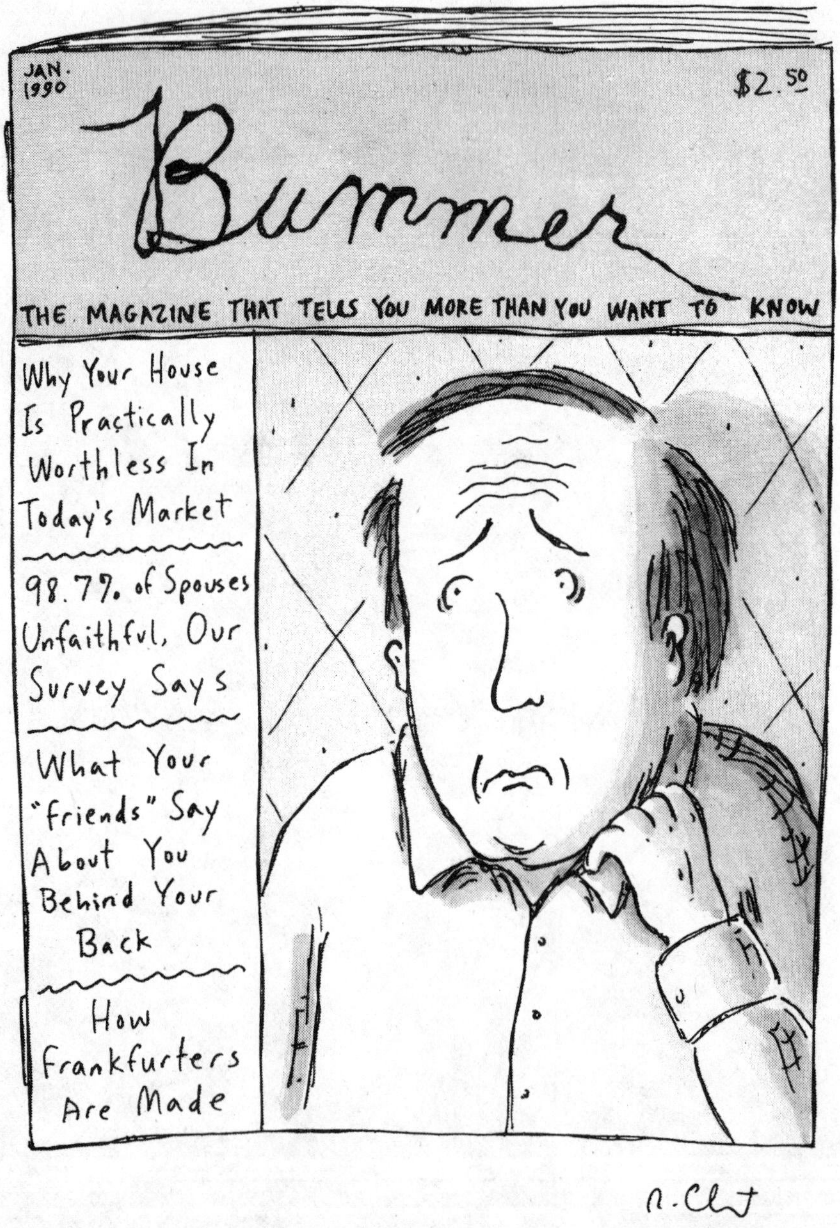
JAN. 1990
$2.50
Bummer
THE MAGAZINE THAT TELLS YOU MORE THAN YOU WANT TO KNOW
Why Your House Is Practically Worthless In Today's Market
98.7% of Spouses Unfaithful, Our Survey Says
What Your "friends" Say About You Behind Your Back
How Frankfurters Are Made
R. Chast

THE TRUE STORY OF
VANILLA PUDDING

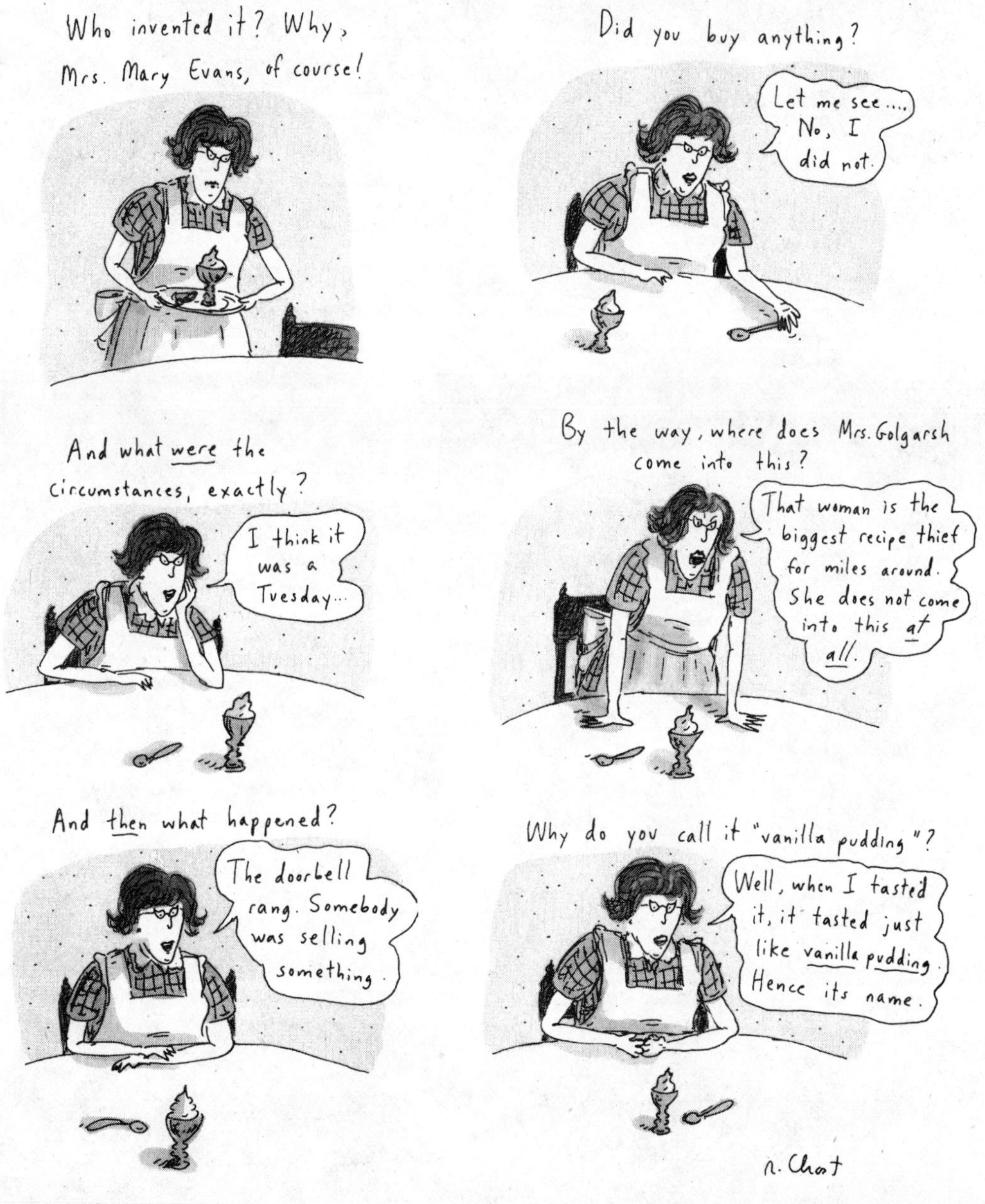

Who invented it? Why, Mrs. Mary Evans, of course!
And what were the circumstances, exactly?
I think it was a Tuesday...
And then what happened?
The doorbell rang. Somebody was selling something.
Did you buy anything?
Let me see.... No, I did not.
By the way, where does Mrs. Golgarsh come into this?
That woman is the biggest recipe thief for miles around. She does not come into this at all.
Why do you call it "vanilla pudding"?
Well, when I tasted it, it tasted just like vanilla pudding. Hence its name.
R. Chast

FROM "THE LETTERS OF JEFFREY FLANDERS AND TIP-TOP UTILITY"

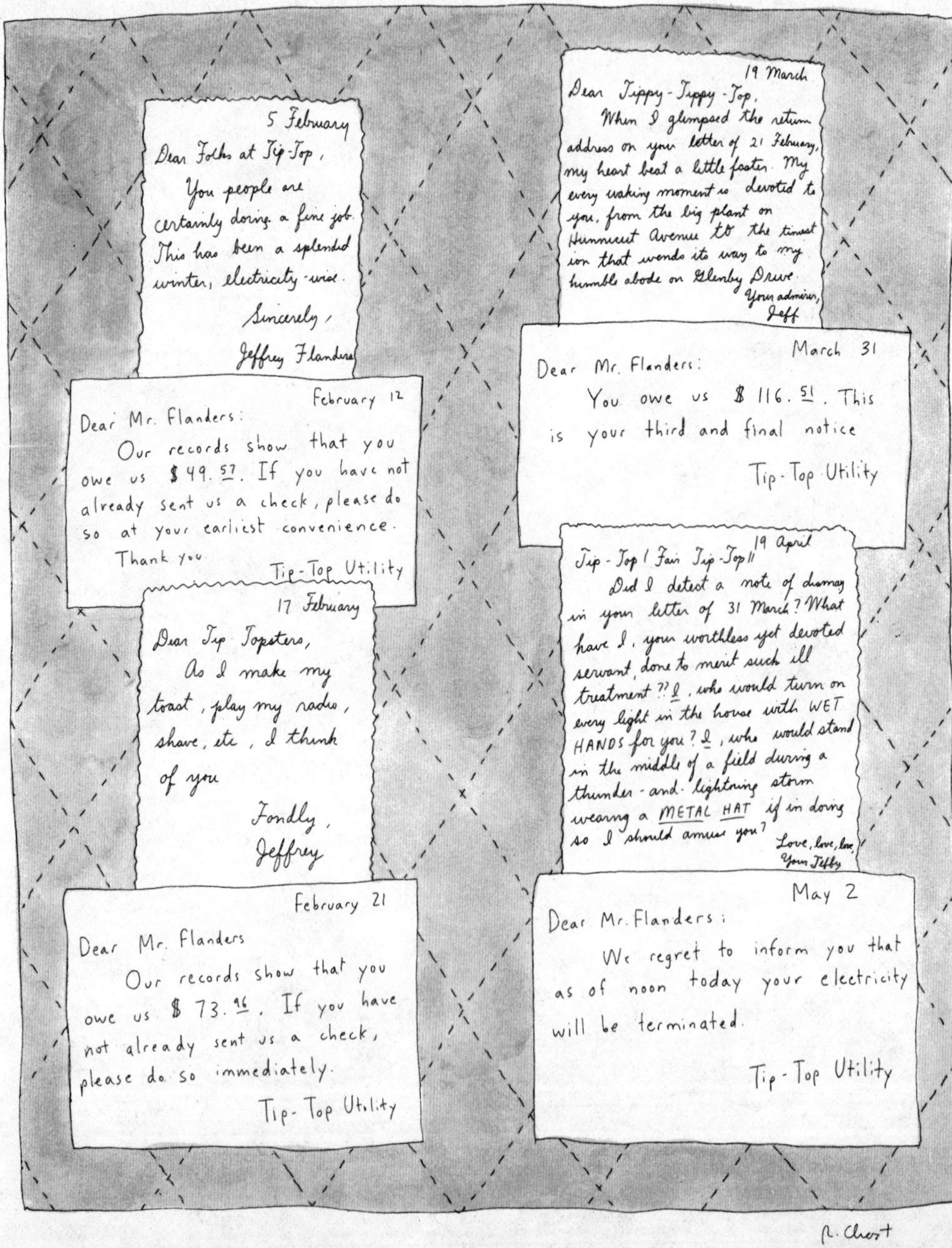
5 February
Dear Folks at Tip-Top,
You people are certainly doing a fine job. This has been a splendid winter, electricity-wise.
Sincerely,
Jeffrey Flanders
February 12
Dear Mr. Flanders:
Our records show that you owe us $49.57. If you have not already sent us a check, please do so at your earliest convenience.
Thank you.
Tip-Top Utility
17 February
Dear Tip Topsters,
As I make my toast, play my radio, shave, etc, I think of you
Fondly,
Jeffrey
February 21
Dear Mr. Flanders
Our records show that you owe us $73.96. If you have not already sent us a check, please do so immediately.
Tip-Top Utility
19 March
Dear Tippy-Tippy-Top,
When I glimpsed the return address on your letter of 21 February, my heart beat a little faster. My every waking moment is devoted to you, from the big plant on Hunnicut Avenue to the tiniest ion that wends its way to my humble abode on Glenby Drive.
Your admirer,
Jeff
March 31
Dear Mr. Flanders:
You owe us $116.51. This is your third and final notice
Tip-Top Utility
19 April
Tip-Top! Fair Tip-Top!!
Did I detect a note of dismay in your letter of 31 March? What have I, your worthless yet devoted servant, done to merit such ill treatment?! I, who would turn on every light in the house with WET HANDS for you? I, who would stand in the middle of a field during a thunder-and-lightning storm wearing a METAL HAT if in doing so I should amuse you?
Love, love, love
Your Jeffy
May 2
Dear Mr. Flanders:
We regret to inform you that as of noon today your electricity will be terminated.
Tip-Top Utility
R. Chast

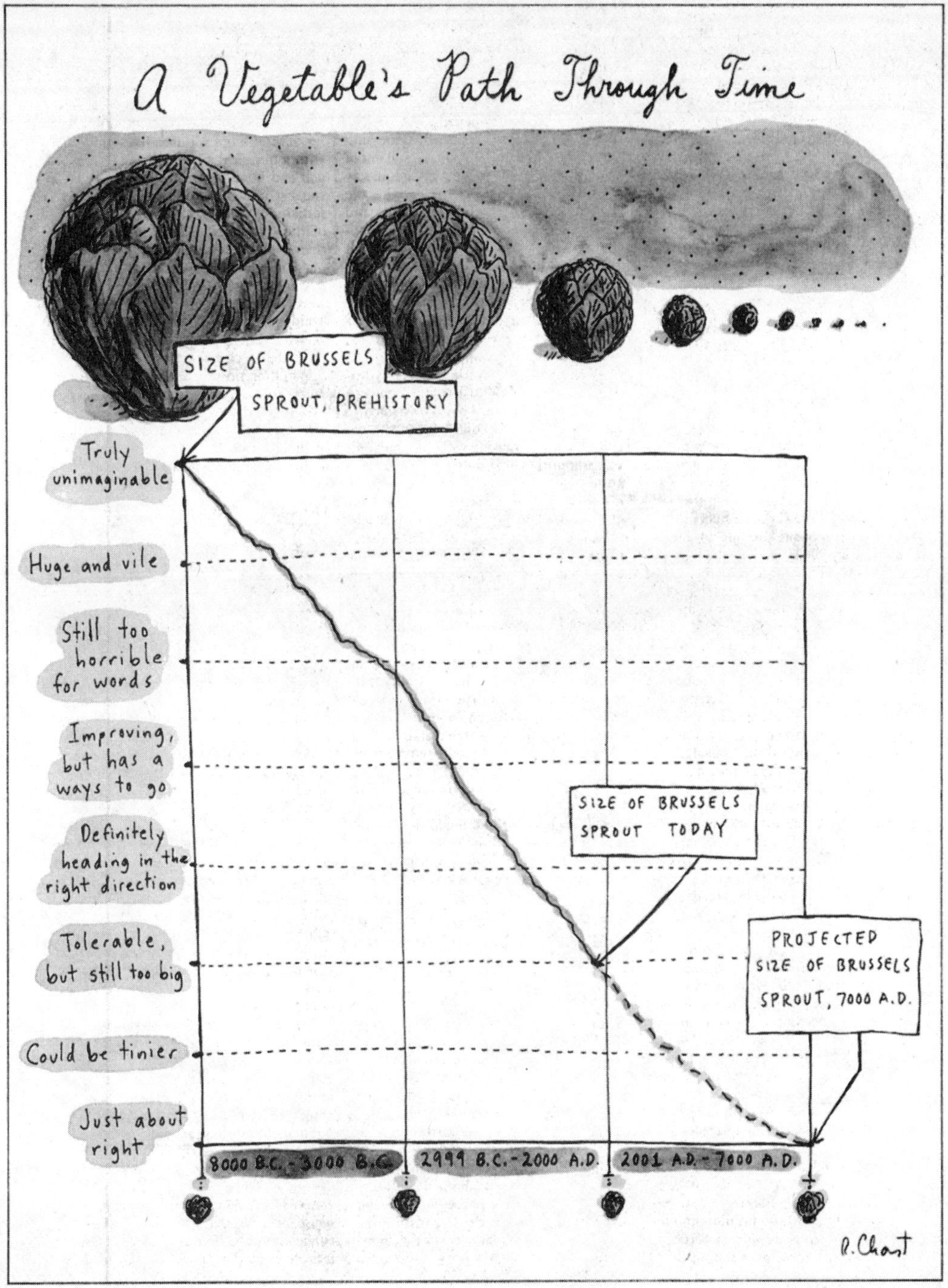
A Vegetable's Path Through Time
SIZE OF BRUSSELS SPROUT, PREHISTORY
Truly unimaginable
Huge and vile
Still too horrible for words
Improving, but has a ways to go
Definitely heading in the right direction
Tolerable, but still too big
Could be tinier
Just about right
SIZE OF BRUSSELS SPROUT TODAY
PROJECTED SIZE OF BRUSSELS SPROUT, 7000 A.D.
8000 B.C.-3000 B.C.
2999 B.C.-2000 A.D.
2001 A.D.-7000 A.D.
R. Chast

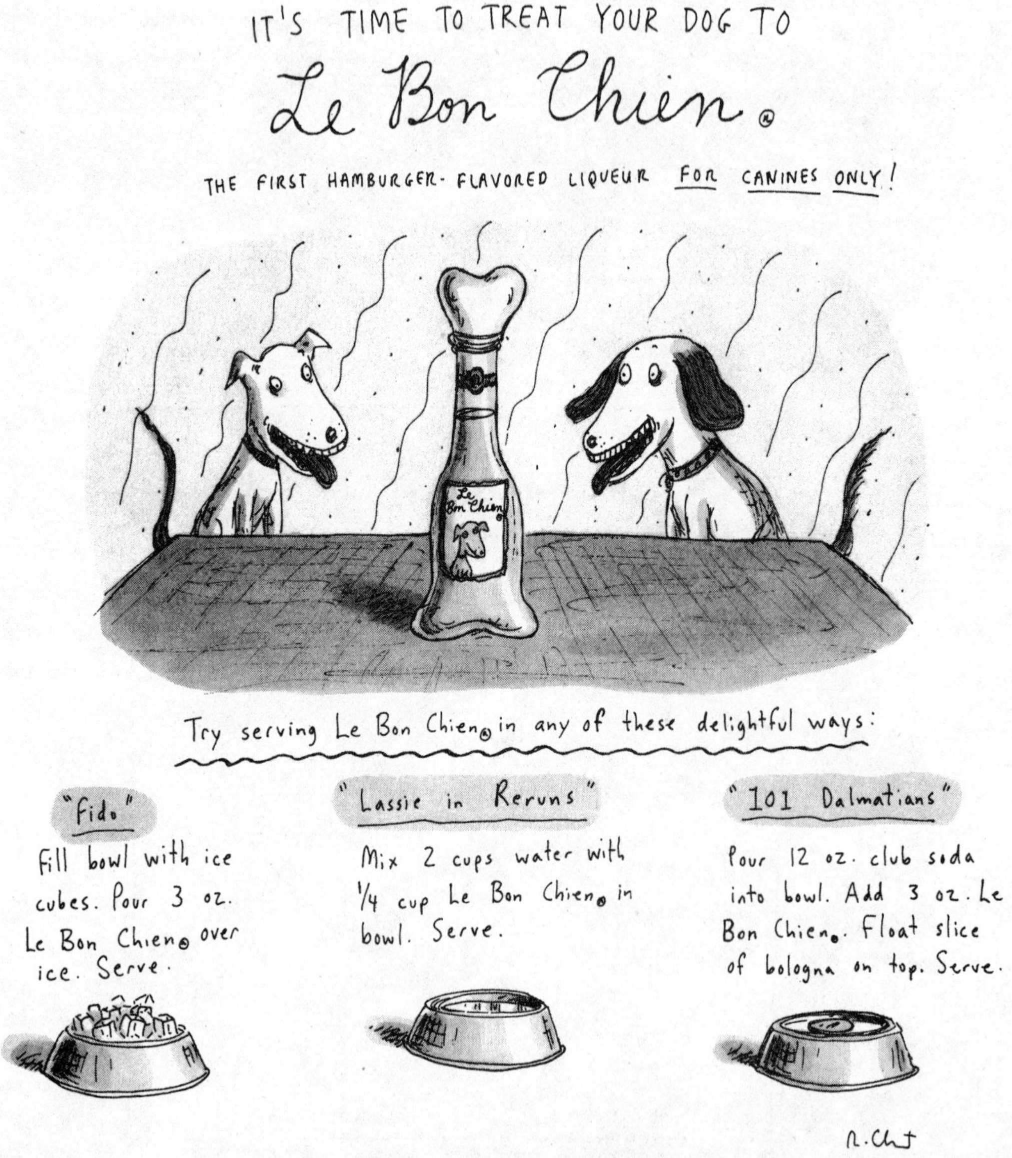
IT'S TIME TO TREAT YOUR DOG TO
Le Bon Chien®
THE FIRST HAMBURGER-FLAVORED LIQUEUR FOR CANINES ONLY!
Le Bon Chien
Try serving Le Bon Chien® in any of these delightful ways:
"Fido"
Fill bowl with ice cubes. Pour 3 oz. Le Bon Chien® over ice. Serve.
"Lassie in Reruns"
Mix 2 cups water with 1/4 cup Le Bon Chien® in bowl. Serve.
"101 Dalmatians"
Pour 12 oz. club soda into bowl. Add 3 oz. Le Bon Chien®. Float slice of bologna on top. Serve.

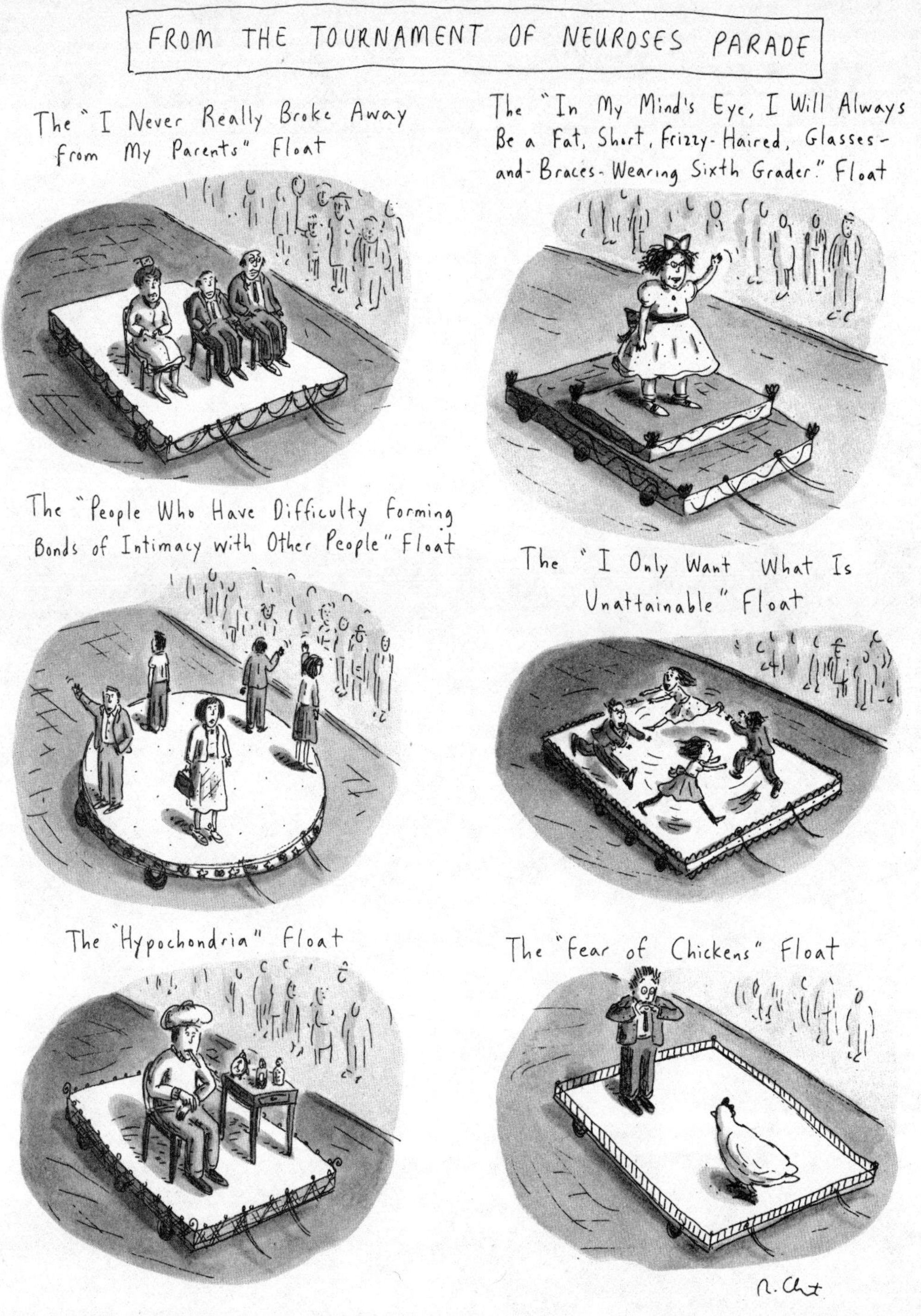
FROM THE TOURNAMENT OF NEUROSES PARADE
The "I Never Really Broke Away from My Parents" Float
The "In My Mind's Eye, I Will Always Be a Fat, Short, Frizzy-Haired, Glasses-and-Braces-Wearing Sixth Grader." Float
The "People Who Have Difficulty Forming Bonds of Intimacy with Other People" Float
The "I Only Want What Is Unattainable" Float
The "Hypochondria" Float
The "Fear of Chickens" Float

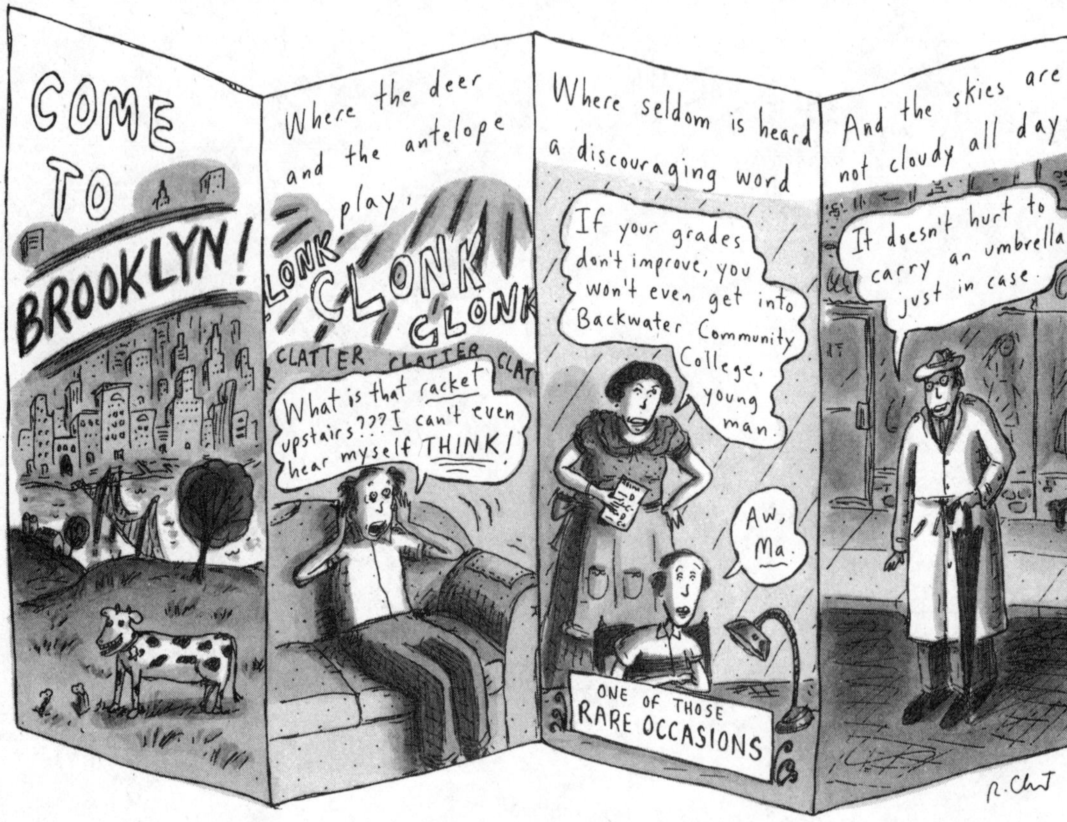
COME TO BROOKLYN!
Where the deer and the antelope play,
LONK CLONK CLONK
CLATTER CLATTER CLAT
What is that racket upstairs???I can't even hear myself THINK!
Where seldom is heard a discouraging word
If your grades don't improve, you won't even get into Backwater Community College, young man.
Aw, Ma.
ONE OF THOSE RARE OCCASIONS
And the skies are not cloudy all day.
It doesn't hurt to carry an umbrella, just in case.
R. Chast

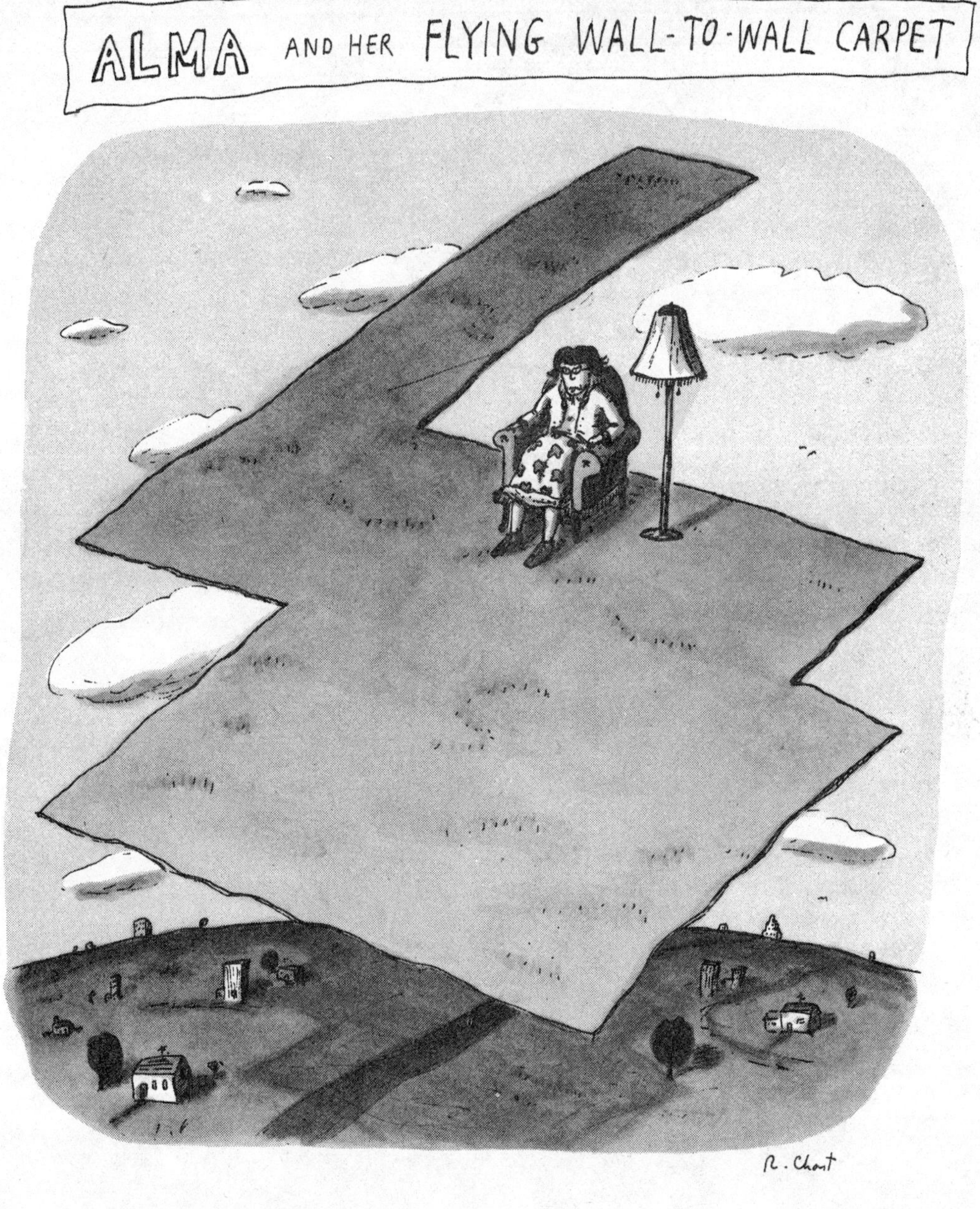
ALMA AND HER FLYING WALL-TO-WALL CARPET
R. Chast

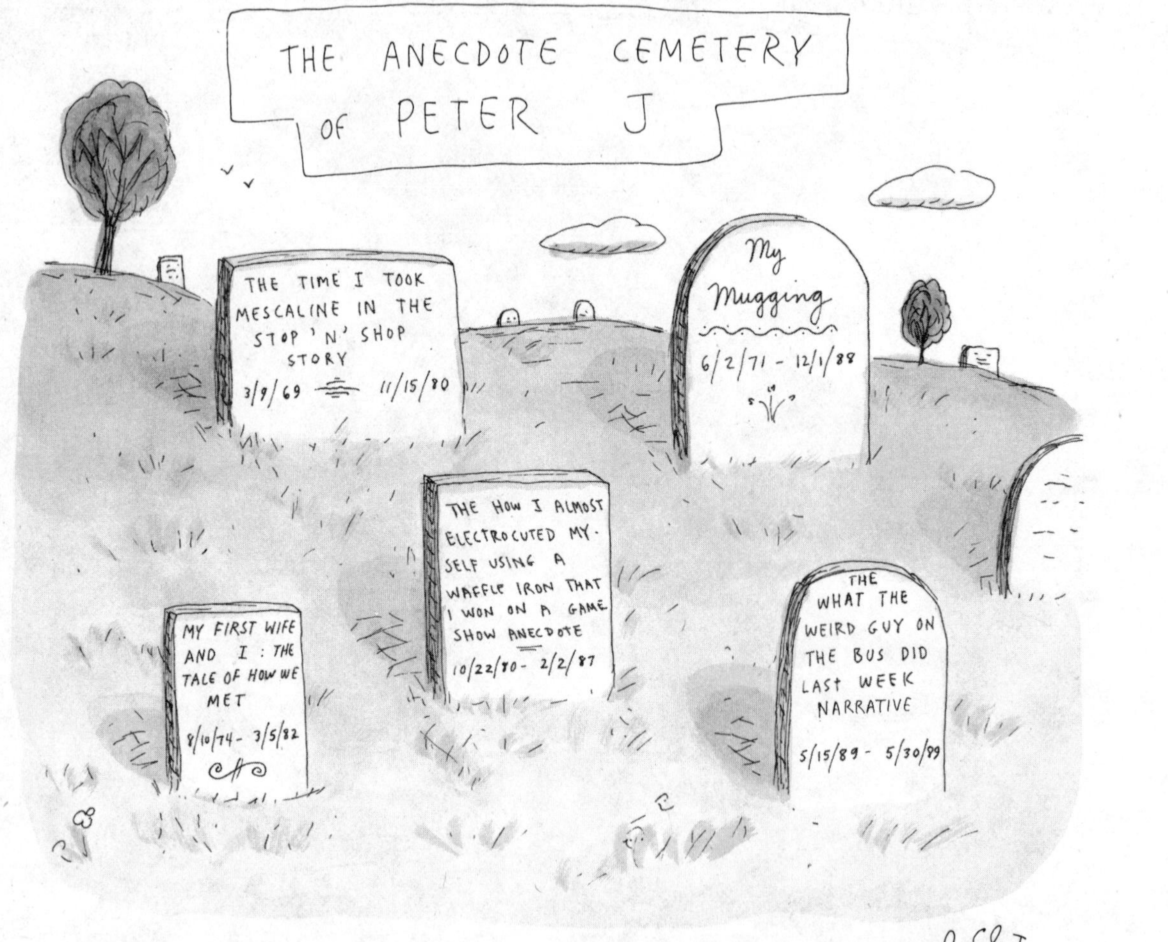
THE ANECDOTE CEMETERY OF PETER J
THE TIME I TOOK MESCALINE IN THE STOP 'N' SHOP STORY
3/9/69 11/15/80
My Mugging
6/2/71 - 12/1/88
THE HOW I ALMOST ELECTROCUTED MYSELF USING A WAFFLE IRON THAT I WON ON A GAME SHOW ANECDOTE
10/22/80 - 2/2/87
MY FIRST WIFE AND I : THE TALE OF HOW WE MET
8/10/74 - 3/5/82
THE WHAT THE WEIRD GUY ON THE BUS DID LAST WEEK NARRATIVE
5/15/89 - 5/30/89
R. Ch

WHY OIL SPILLS ARE GOOD

BY D. ALVIN ARMBRUSTER, C.E.O., ABC OIL CORPORATION

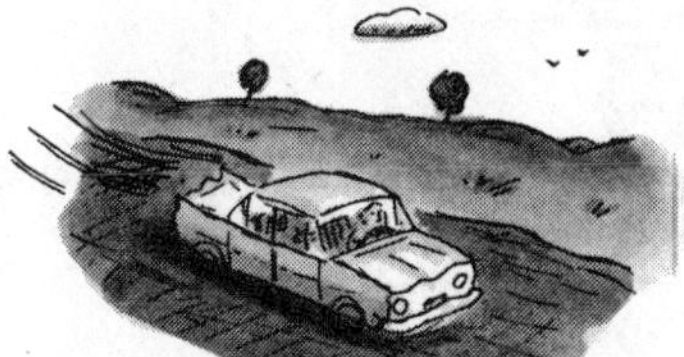

①

EVERY ONCE IN A WHILE, IT'S GOOD TO GIVE THE OCEANS' SELF-CLEANING MECHANISMS A REAL WORKOUT. IT'S LIKE TAKING YOUR CAR FOR A LONG, FAST DRIVE ON A SUMMER AFTERNOON.

②

OIL-COATED BIRDS ARE BETTER PROTECTED AGAINST THE SUN'S RAYS THAN NON-OIL-COATED BIRDS.

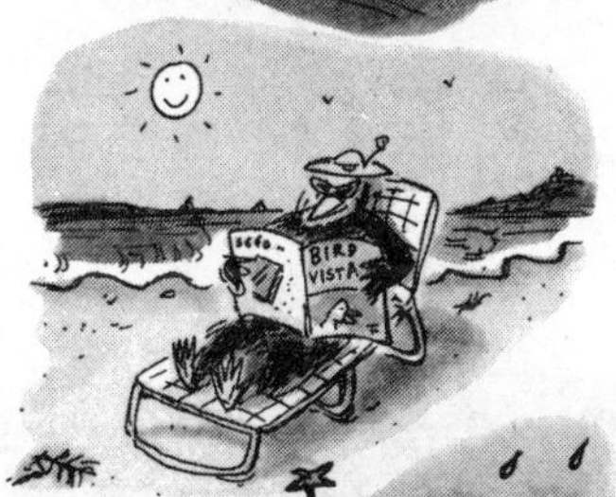
BIRD VISTA

③

LAB TESTS PROVE THAT MANY UNDERWATER PLANTS ACTUALLY *LOVE* THE TASTE OF PETROLEUM!

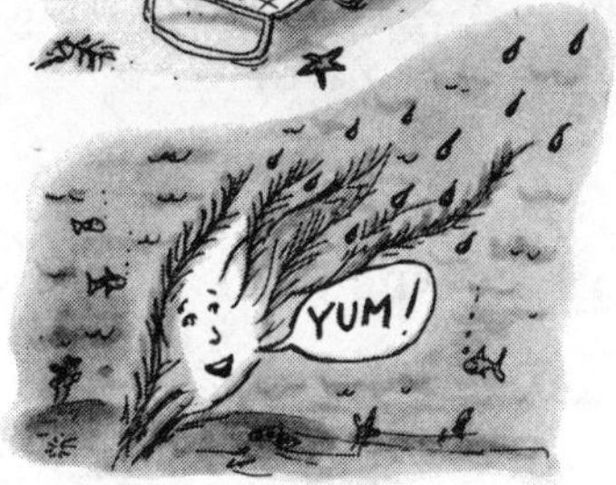
YUM!

④

A RUINED FISHING INDUSTRY MEANS THAT PEOPLE WILL GO BACK TO EATING MORE MEAT, AMERICA'S MOST VIRILE FOOD.

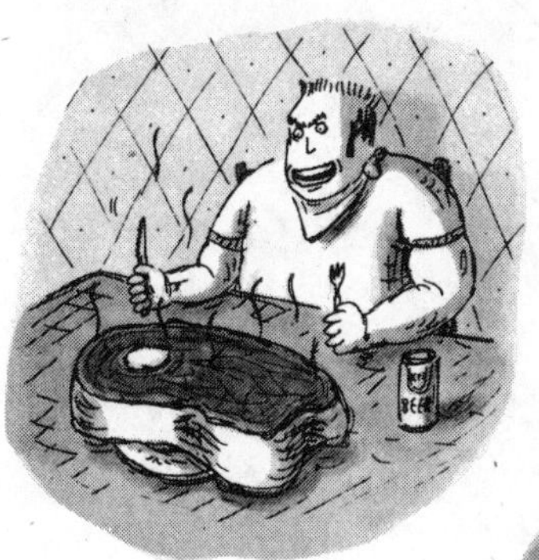

⑤

PEOPLE IN THE MEDIA ALSO BENEFIT! SPILL-VIDEOTAPERS, INTERVIEWERS OF BIRD-WASHERS, ECOLOGICAL-DISASTER PREDICTORS, ETC.— WITHOUT US, WHERE WOULD *THEY* BE?

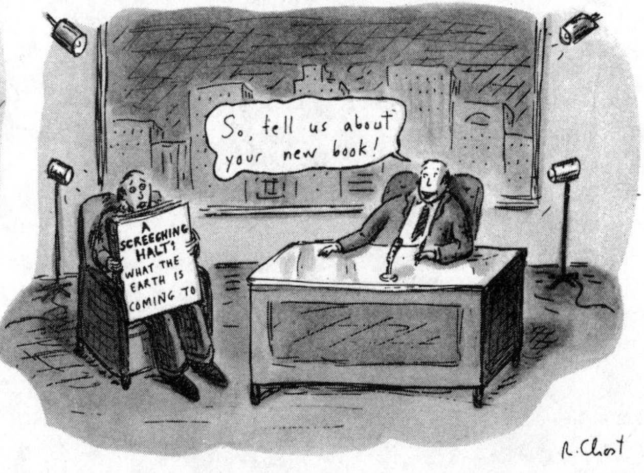
So, tell us about your new book!
A SCREECHING HALT: WHAT THE EARTH IS COMING TO

R. Chast

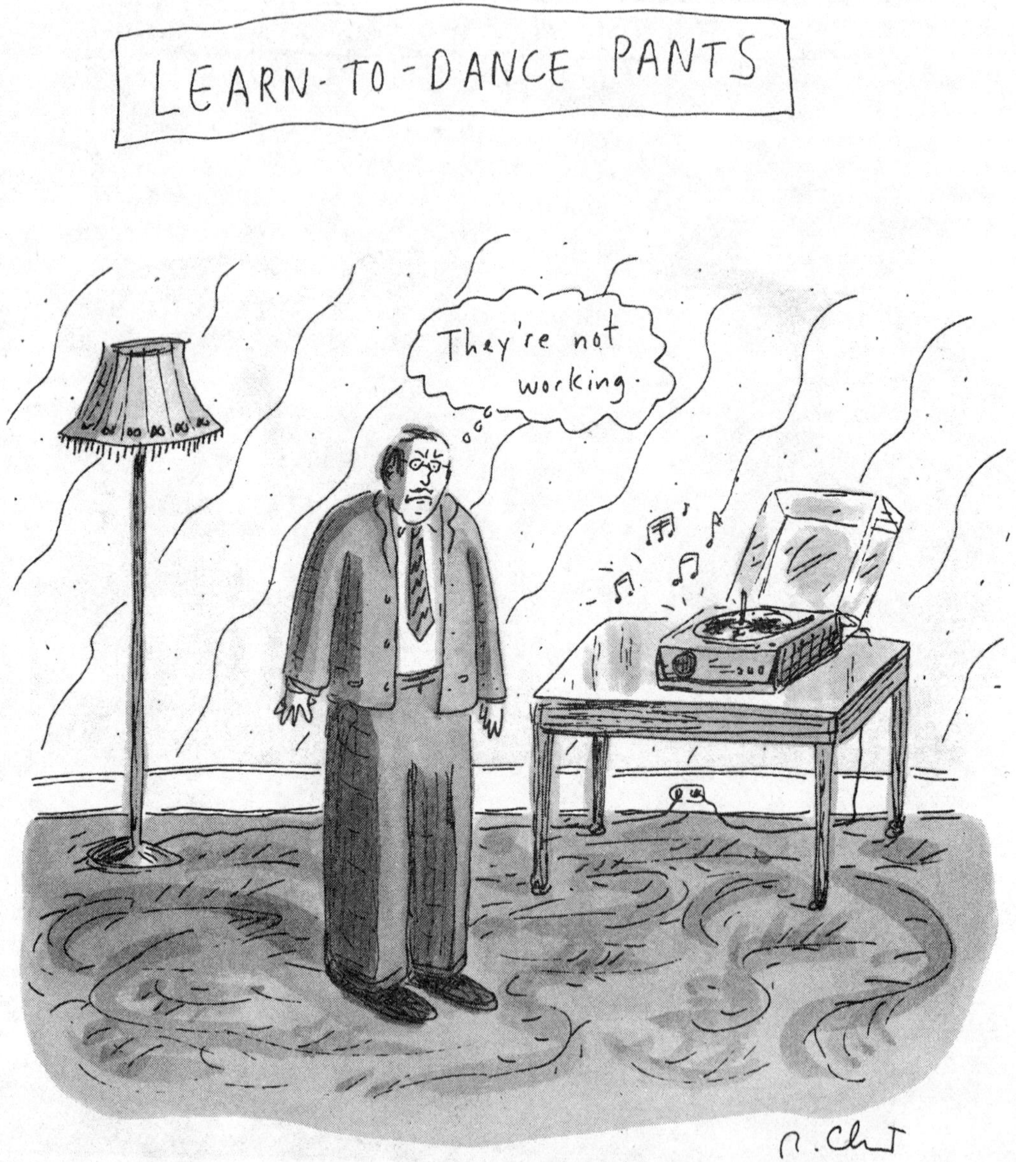
LEARN-TO-DANCE PANTS
They're not working.

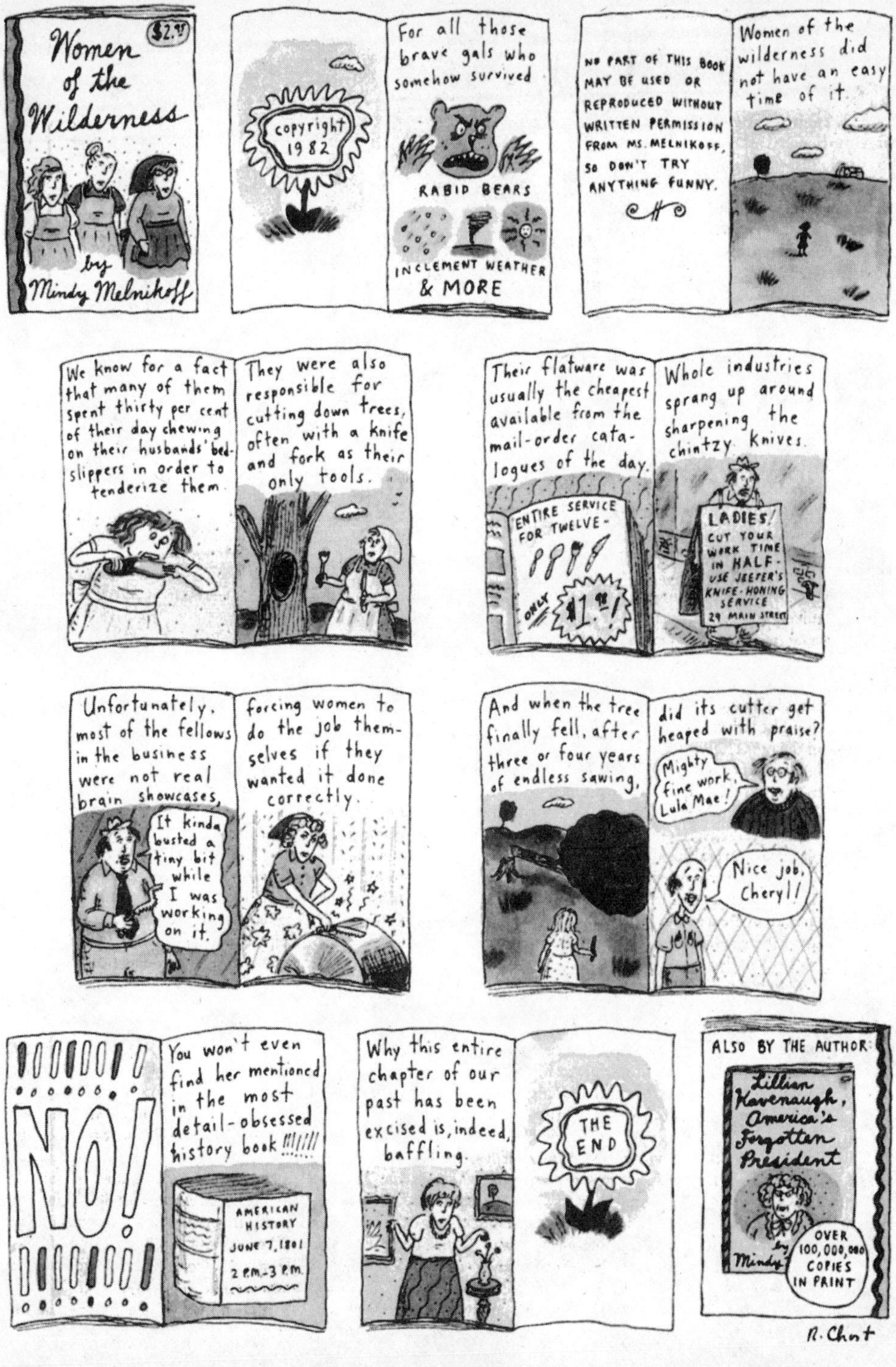

Women of the Wilderness
$2.95
by Mindy Melnikoff
copyright 1982
For all those brave gals who somehow survived
RABID BEARS
INCLEMENT WEATHER
& MORE
NO PART OF THIS BOOK MAY BE USED OR REPRODUCED WITHOUT WRITTEN PERMISSION FROM MS. MELNIKOFF, SO DON'T TRY ANYTHING FUNNY.
Women of the wilderness did not have an easy time of it.
We know for a fact that many of them spent thirty per cent of their day chewing on their husbands' bed-slippers in order to tenderize them.
They were also responsible for cutting down trees, often with a knife and fork as their only tools.
Their flatware was usually the cheapest available from the mail-order catalogues of the day.
ENTIRE SERVICE FOR TWELVE-
ONLY $1.98!
Whole industries sprang up around sharpening the chintzy knives.
LADIES! CUT YOUR WORK TIME IN HALF- USE JEEFER'S KNIFE-HONING SERVICE 29 MAIN STREET
Unfortunately, most of the fellows in the business were not real brain showcases,
It kinda busted a tiny bit while I was working on it.
forcing women to do the job themselves if they wanted it done correctly.
And when the tree finally fell, after three or four years of endless sawing,
did its cutter get heaped with praise?
Mighty fine work, Lula Mae!
Nice job, Cheryl!
NO!
You won't even find her mentioned in the most detail-obsessed history book!!!!!!
AMERICAN HISTORY JUNE 7, 1801 2 P.M.-3 P.M.
Why this entire chapter of our past has been excised is, indeed, baffling.
THE END
ALSO BY THE AUTHOR:
Lillian Kavenaugh, America's Forgotten President
by Mindy
OVER 100,000,000 COPIES IN PRINT
R. Chast

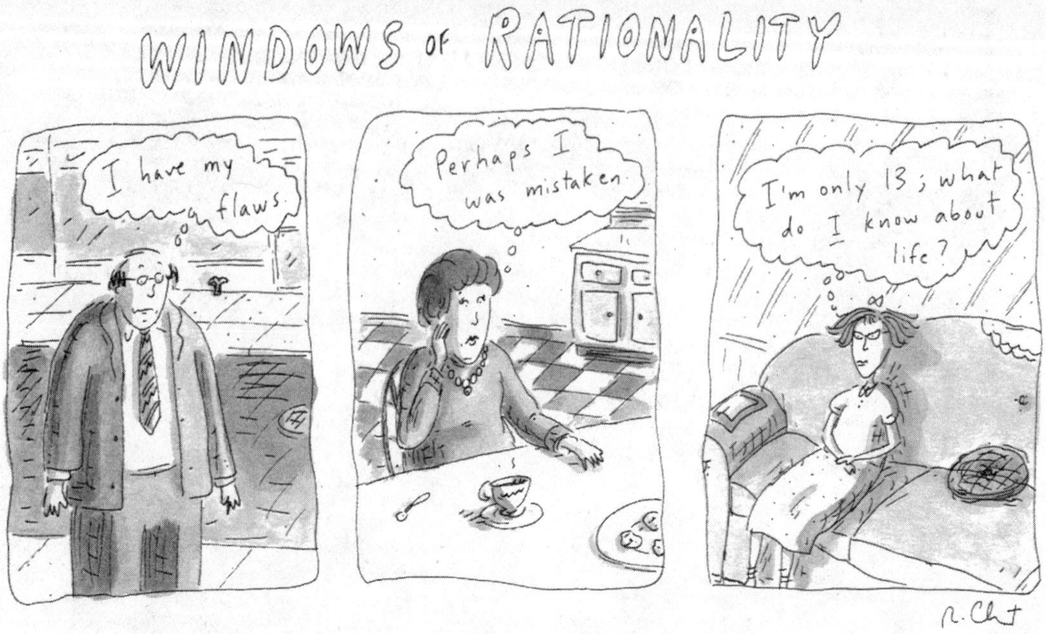
WINDOWS OF RATIONALITY
I have my flaws.
Perhaps I was mistaken.
I'm only 13; what do I know about life?
R. Chast

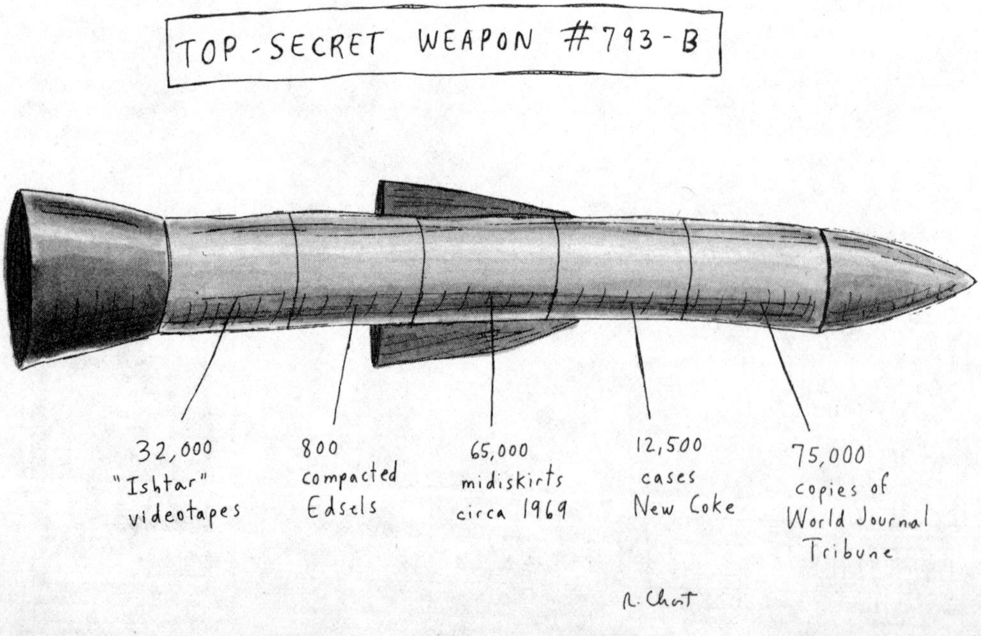
TOP-SECRET WEAPON #793-B
32,000 "Ishtar" videotapes
800 compacted Edsels
65,000 midiskirts circa 1969
12,500 cases New Coke
75,000 copies of World Journal Tribune
R. Chast

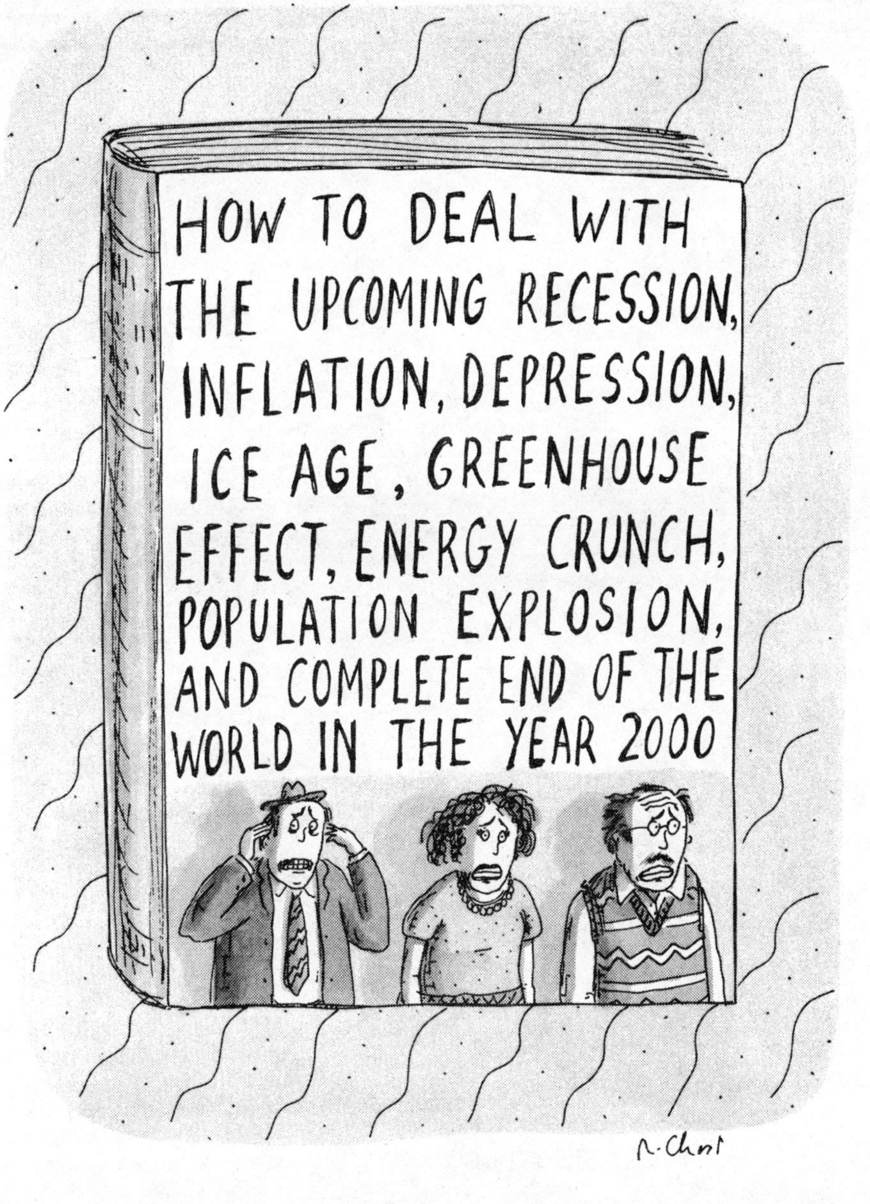
HOW TO DEAL WITH THE UPCOMING RECESSION, INFLATION, DEPRESSION, ICE AGE, GREENHOUSE EFFECT, ENERGY CRUNCH, POPULATION EXPLOSION, AND COMPLETE END OF THE WORLD IN THE YEAR 2000

THE TRIUMPH OF SUBSTANCE OVER STYLE

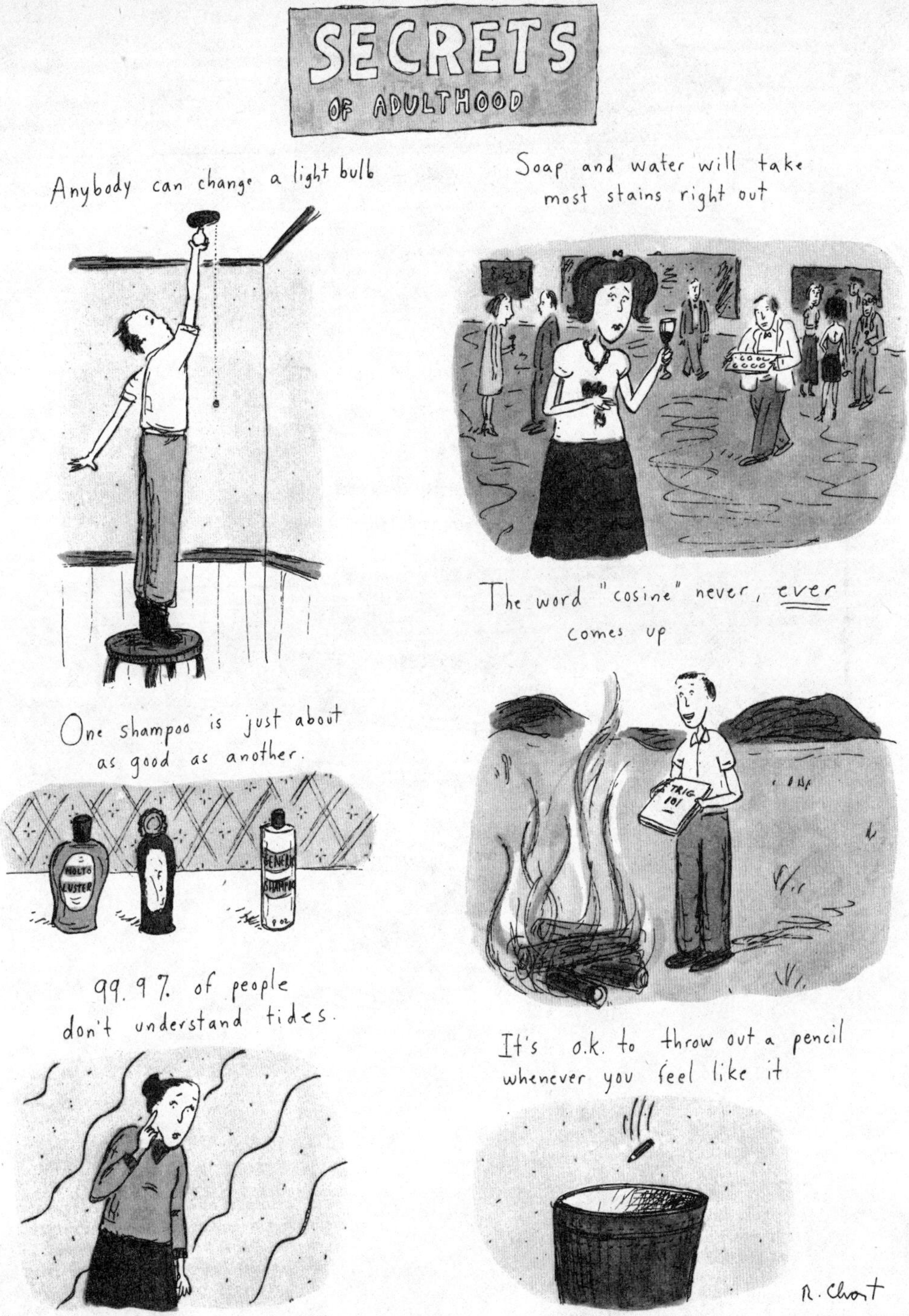
SECRETS OF ADULTHOOD
Anybody can change a light bulb
Soap and water will take most stains right out
The word "cosine" never, ever comes up
TRIG 101
One shampoo is just about as good as another.
MOLTO LUSTER
99.9% of people don't understand tides.
It's o.k. to throw out a pencil whenever you feel like it
R. Chast

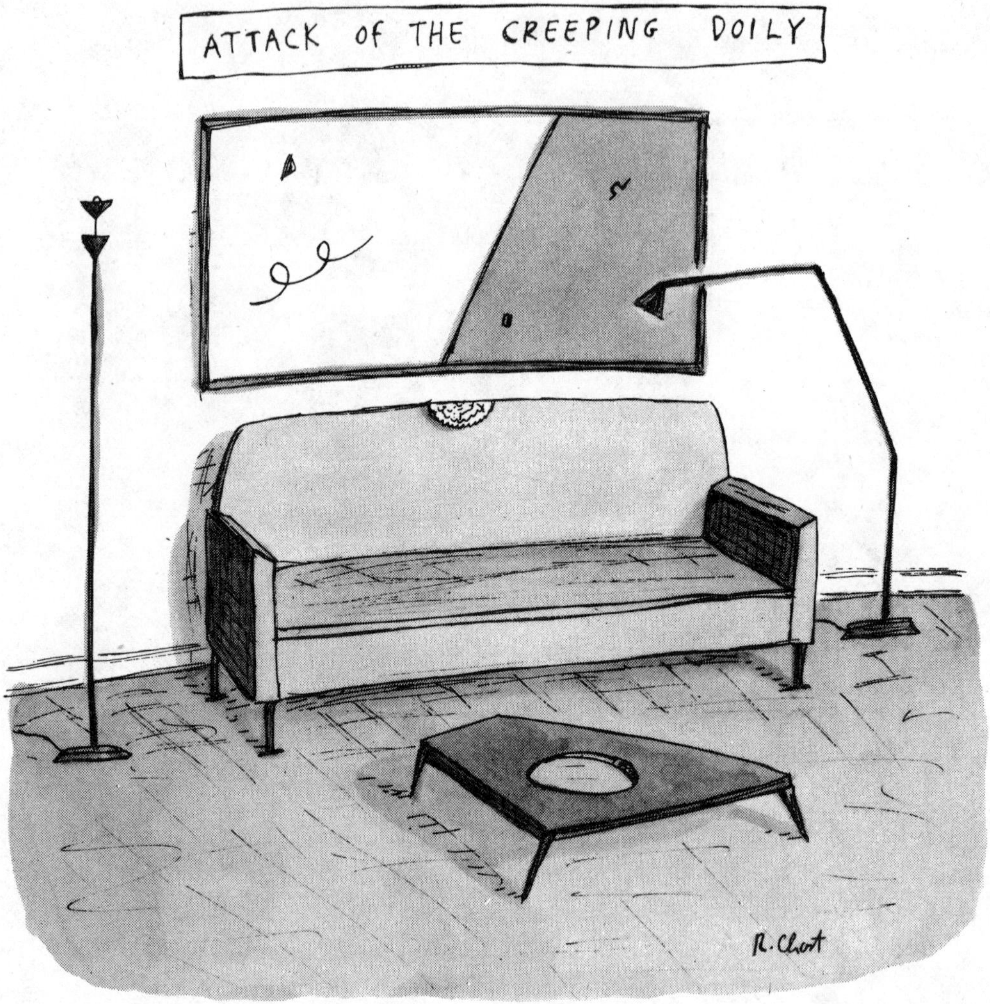
ATTACK OF THE CREEPING DOILY
R. Chast

HADLEY K., ALL-DAY SUCKER

8:00 A.M. ~ Woke up. Ate oat bran followed by tons of vitamins.

8:37 A.M. ~ Called and pledged $100.⁰⁰ to the Your Condo in Heaven Foundation.

9:12 A.M. ~ Went outside, played a little three-card monte

11:00 A.M. ~ Attended "Vortex Mind Control" Seminar at New York Penta.

12:39 P.M. ~ Bought Cartier watch from street vender.

1:00 P.M. ~ Lunch: paid $19.⁰⁰ for spaghetti and meatballs.

2:02 P.M. ~ Bought Vuitton luggage from street vender.

2:26 P.M. ~ Went home; talked to Aunt Shelley; got into argument over whether or not she was thanked for socks she gave me four years ago, let her win.

3:00 P.M. ~ Aromatherapy class.

5:21 P.M. ~ Gave money to guy collecting for the Save the Chrysler Building Foundation.

7:00 P.M. ~ Dinner: paid $35.⁰⁰ for hamburger and French fries.

8:18 P.M. ~ Went home. Agreed to write 50,000-word article on cold fusion for $25.⁰⁰.

9:09 P.M. ~ Ordered shoes from a catalogue.

10:36 P.M. ~ Read book on channelling.

12:11 A.M. ~ Slept on special orthopedic pillow while listening to "Learn French Overnight" cassette.

R. Chast

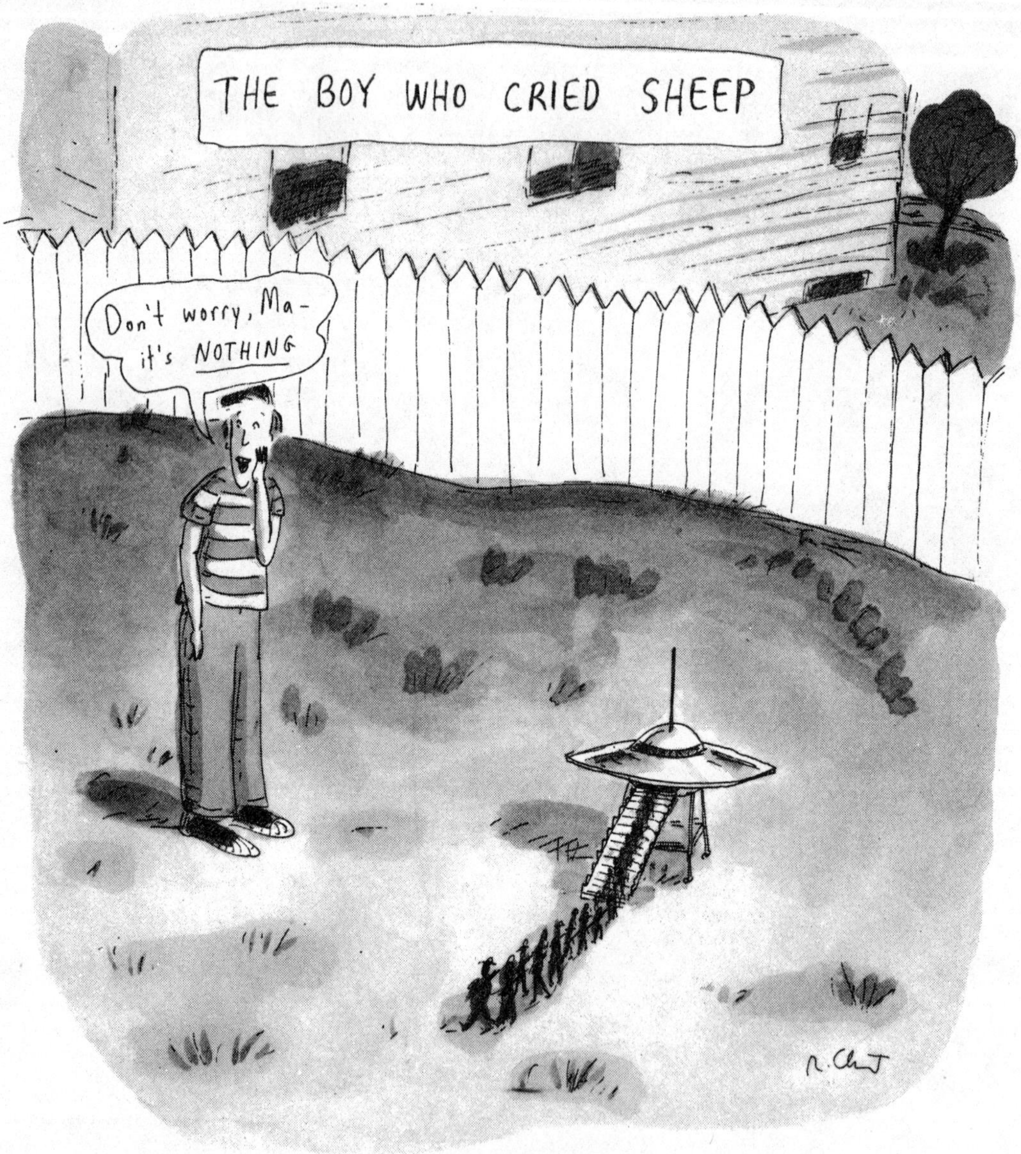
THE BOY WHO CRIED SHEEP
Don't worry, Ma- it's NOTHING
R. Chast

FOR THE NEW GARDENER

#3017 Plant Comb and Brush Set —
Keep your greenery looking spry. Order now and we'll throw in some shampoo.

$22.00

#4629 Specialty Shovels —
You don't really need these, and you don't even know what they're for, do you? Go ahead, get them anyway.

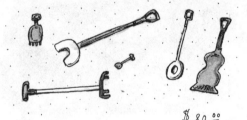

$80.00

#5780 Expert Gardener's Outfit —
Once you get the "look" right, everything else will surely fall into place.

professional gardener's hat

old clothes

special clogs

$195.00

#6338 Anti-Dandelion Cassette —
Voice intones, "Dandelions, BEGONE!" for 90 minutes. The results will astonish you.

$10.00

#8028 Low-Fat Plant Food —
If you care at all about your plants, this is what you'll feed them.

Methuselah LOW-FAT PLANT FOOD

MIX WITH WATER

$7.50

#9976 Glue-on Flowers —
For when all else fails.

BEFORE   AFTER

$18.00

r.Cht

OVERPRIVILEGED CHECKING*

(* FOR THOSE WITH ASSETS OVER $500,000,000,000.⁰⁰)

Our "Get It All Off Your Chest®" service~ Come on in and yell at the employee of your choice for no reason at all. That's what they're there for!

Our "Drive Through Doors ®" service~ So it's not a regular "drive-through" bank. Who cares? It is for you!

Our "Whatever You Want to Know®" service~ In a snoopy mood? Feel free to page through customers' account records! Fascinating stuff!!

R. Chast

The Hanging Gardens

Magnetic Field

A Hot Spot

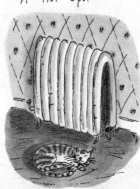

Singing Rocks

A Natural Bridge

r. Chast

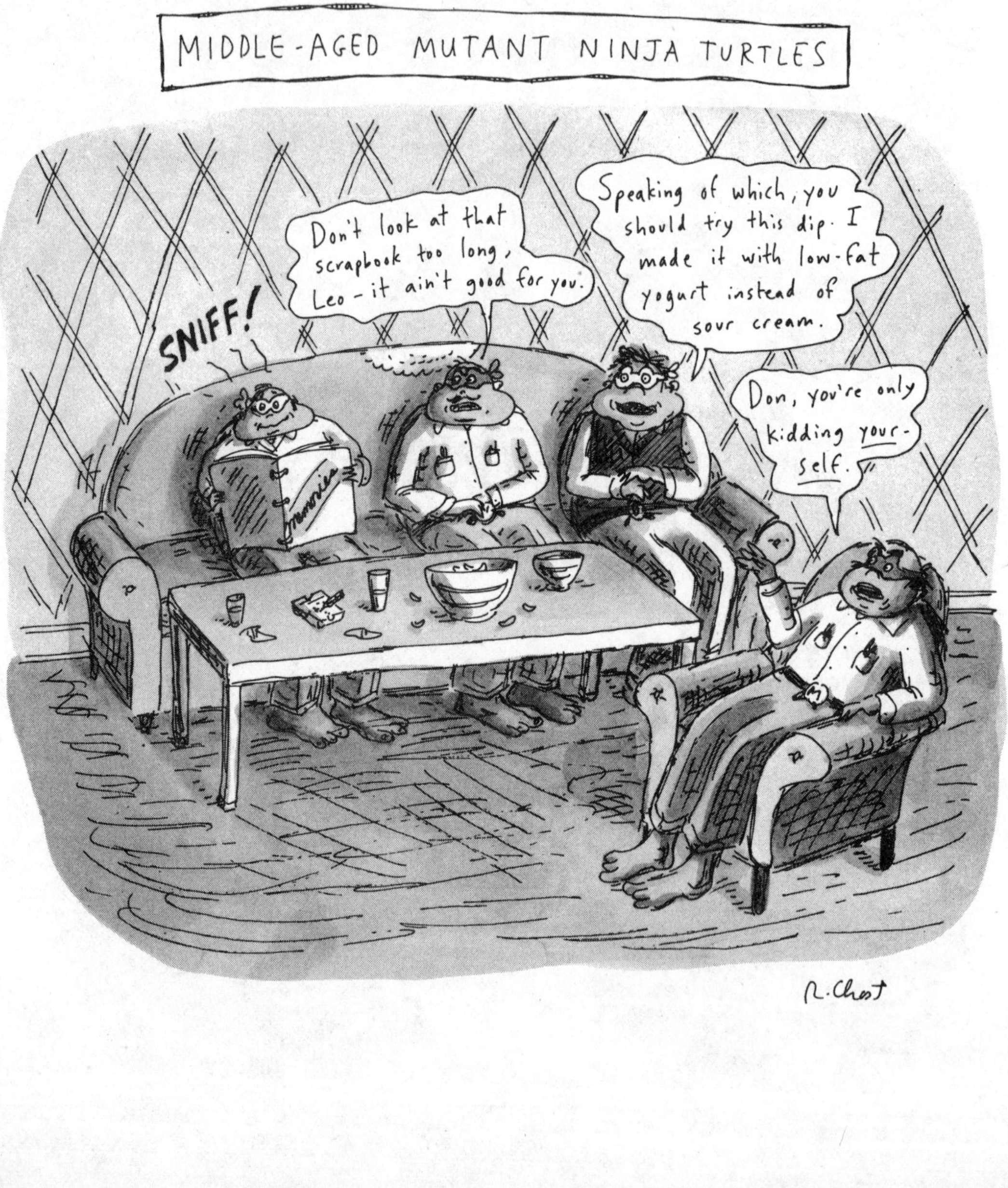
MIDDLE-AGED MUTANT NINJA TURTLES
SNIFF!
Memories
Don't look at that scrapbook too long, Leo - it ain't good for you.
Speaking of which, you should try this dip. I made it with low-fat yogurt instead of sour cream.
Don, you're only kidding your-self.
R. Chast

THANK YOU FOR JOINING THE LIMITED-ATTENTION-SPAN BOOK CLUB HERE IS YOUR FIRST NOVEL:

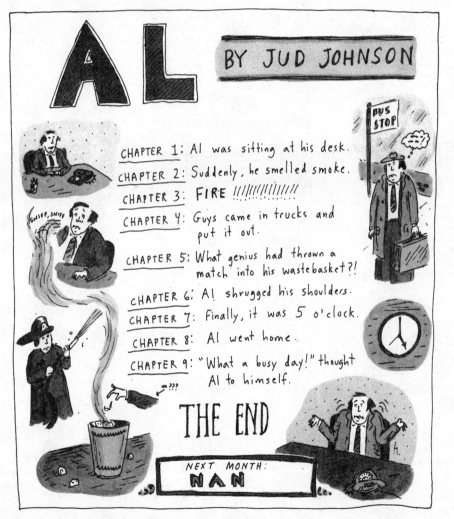

AL
BY JUD JOHNSON

CHAPTER 1: Al was sitting at his desk.

CHAPTER 2: Suddenly, he smelled smoke.

CHAPTER 3: FIRE !!!!!!!!!!!!!!

CHAPTER 4: Guys came in trucks and put it out.

CHAPTER 5: What genius had thrown a match into his wastebasket?!

CHAPTER 6: Al shrugged his shoulders.

CHAPTER 7: Finally, it was 5 o'clock.

CHAPTER 8: Al went home.

CHAPTER 9: "What a busy day!" thought Al to himself.

THE END

NEXT MONTH:
NAN

R. Cht

THE ADVENTURES OF WIMP MOM

There are definitely times of the day when one's three-year-old may be in a horrible mood.
Who knows what the Tough Mom might do to stop that sort of thing?
NOW YOU STAY IN YOUR ROOM UNTIL YOU'RE READY TO ACT LIKE A HUMAN BEING, PAL!!!!!
If you are a Wimp Mom, perhaps you will try to distract your kid in a calm, soothing manner.
ALL YOU WANT TO KNOW ABOUT DINOSAURS
Honeybunch, let's go over to the couch and READ ABOUT DINOSAURS!
You are lucky if this works for ten seconds.
"Dinosaurs were very, very big."
Often, you will only find yourself in deeper and hotter water.
NO, THEY WEREN'T!!!
What a wimpy, wimpy Mom.
O.K., they weren't big. They were as tiny as peas.

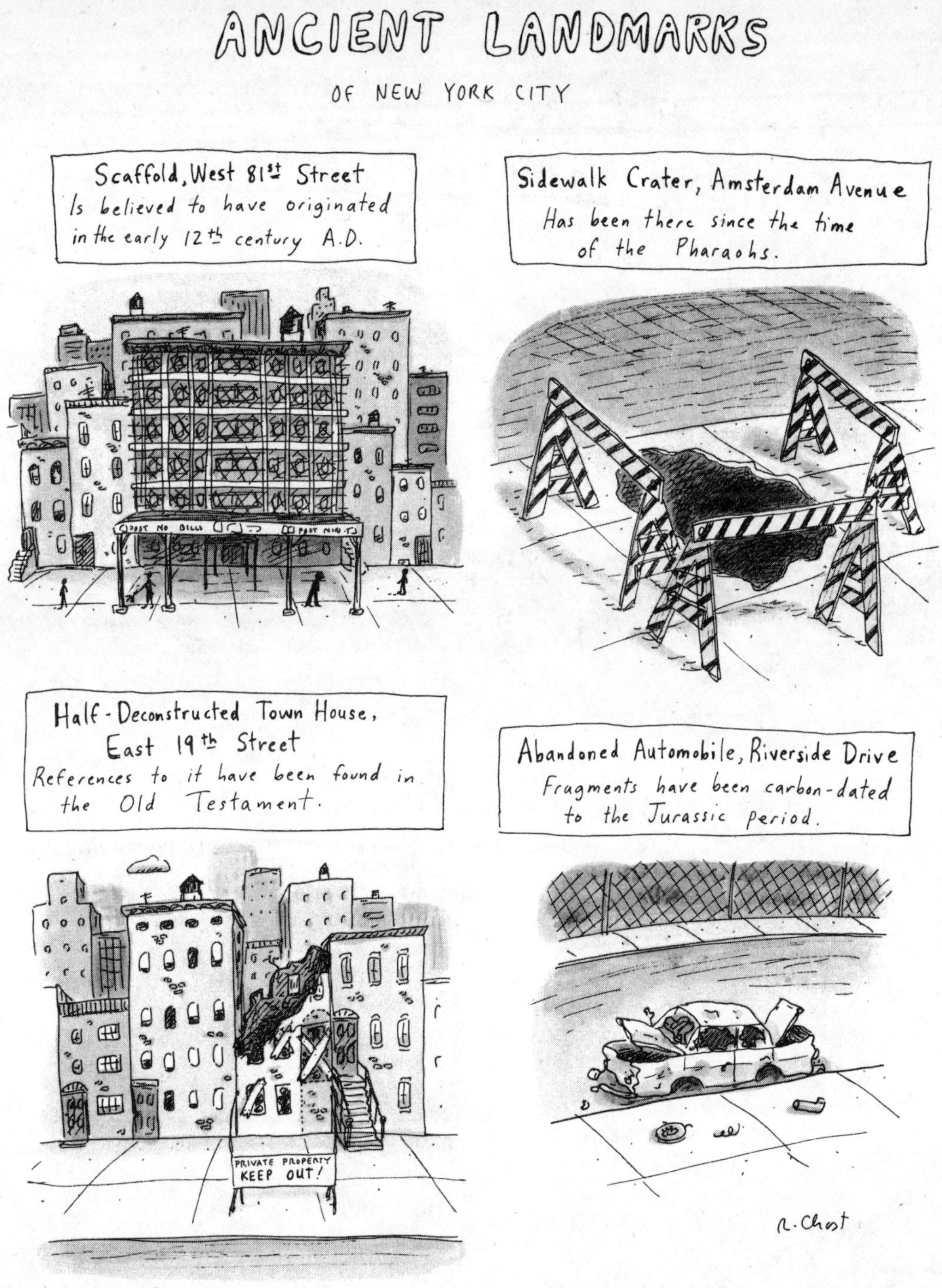
ANCIENT LANDMARKS
OF NEW YORK CITY
Scaffold, West 81st Street
Is believed to have originated in the early 12th century A.D.
POST NO BILLS
Sidewalk Crater, Amsterdam Avenue
Has been there since the time of the Pharaohs.
Half-Deconstructed Town House, East 19th Street
References to it have been found in the Old Testament.
PRIVATE PROPERTY
KEEP OUT!
Abandoned Automobile, Riverside Drive
Fragments have been carbon-dated to the Jurassic period.
R. Chast

FAILED LAUNDRY DETERGENTS

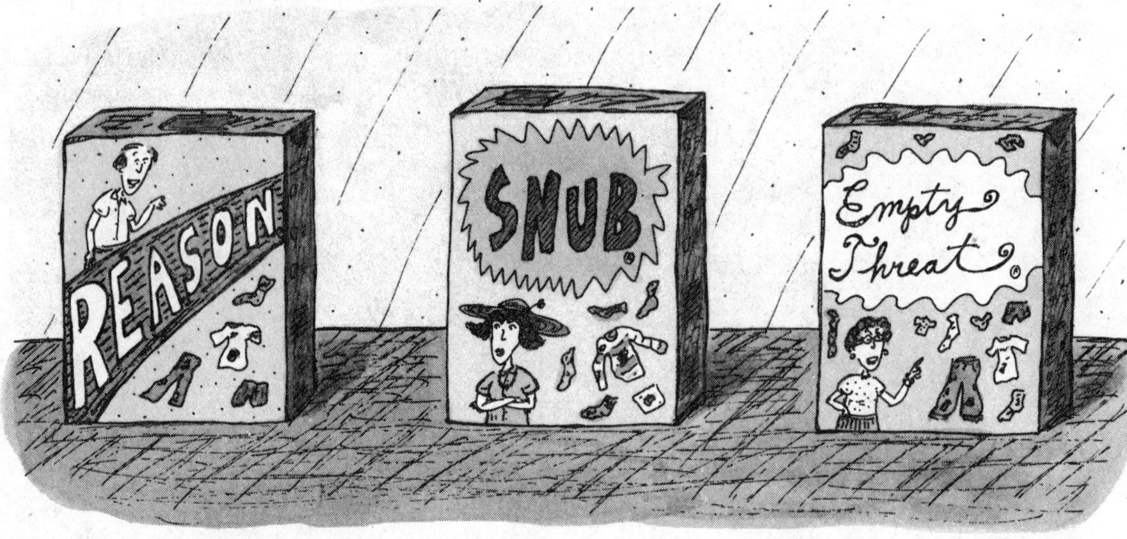
REASON
SNUB
Empty Threat

The detergent that tries to persuade dirt that it really isn't wanted and should therefore leave.

The soap flakes that totally ignore dirt in the hope that it will go away.

The cleanser that tells dirt that unless it dissolves this instant there will be hell to pay.

ENTRANCE EXAM FOR THE
MILDRED SCHOOL OF MEDICINE
CAUSE
EFFECT
1. Sitting on the ground
2. Eating hot dog from street vender
HOT
3. Rubbing eye
4. Wearing sneakers without socks
A. Coma
B. Blindness
C. Insanity
D. A life-sapping malaise that no doctor will ever be able to cure
ANSWERS NEXT WEEK
R. Chast

CROSS-COUNTRY KNITTING

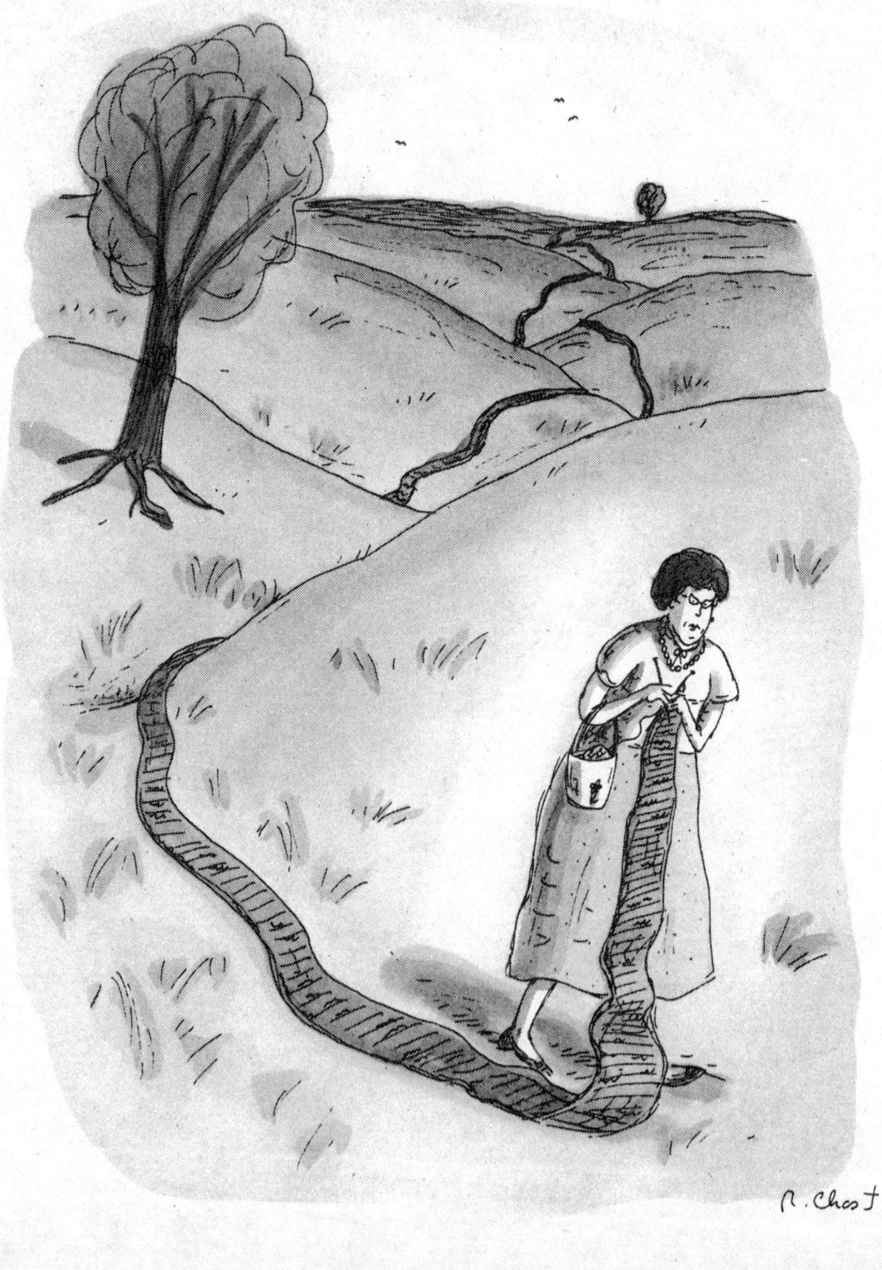
R. Chast

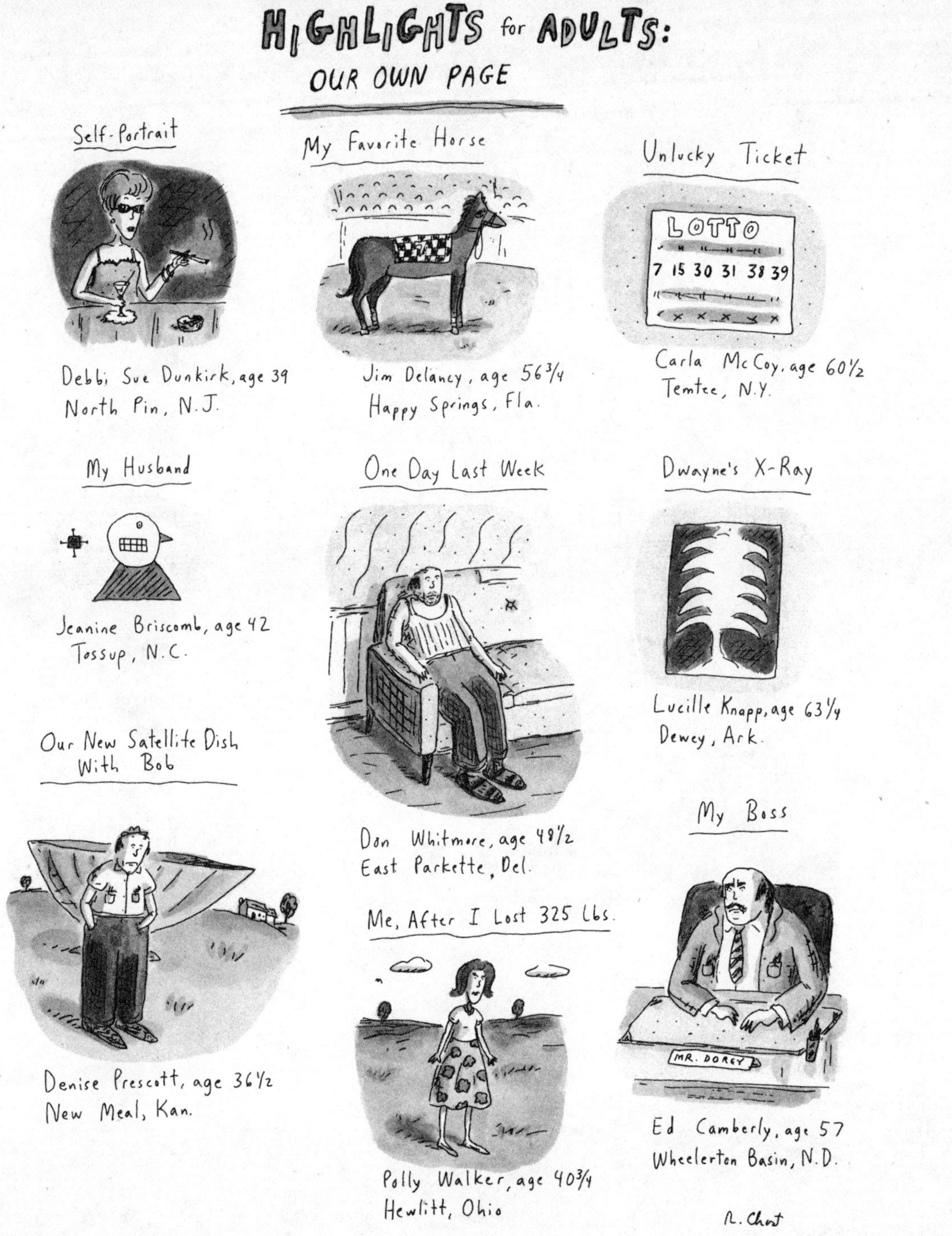
HIGHLIGHTS for ADULTS:
OUR OWN PAGE
Self-Portrait
Debbi Sue Dunkirk, age 39
North Pin, N.J.
My Favorite Horse
Jim Delancy, age 56 3/4
Happy Springs, Fla.
Unlucky Ticket
LOTTO
7 15 30 31 38 39
Carla McCoy, age 60 1/2
Temtee, N.Y.
My Husband
Jeanine Briscomb, age 42
Tossup, N.C.
One Day Last Week
Don Whitmore, age 48 1/2
East Parkette, Del.
Dwayne's X-Ray
Lucille Knapp, age 63 1/4
Dewey, Ark.
Our New Satellite Dish With Bob
Denise Prescott, age 36 1/2
New Meal, Kan.
Me, After I Lost 325 Lbs.
Polly Walker, age 40 3/4
Hewlitt, Ohio
My Boss
MR. DOREY
Ed Camberly, age 57
Wheelerton Basin, N.D.
R. Chast

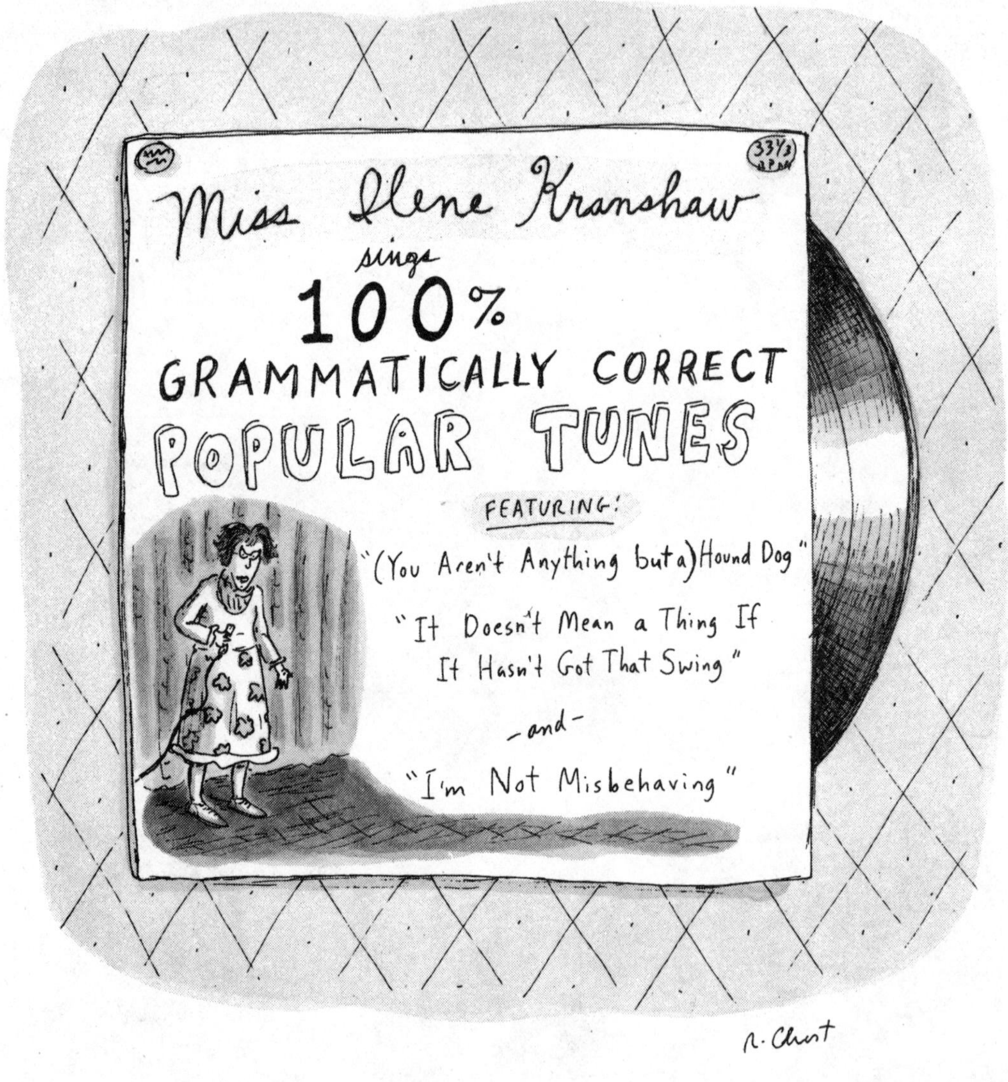

33⅓ RPM
Miss Ilene Kranshaw
sings
100%
GRAMMATICALLY CORRECT
POPULAR TUNES
FEATURING:
"(You Aren't Anything but a) Hound Dog"
"It Doesn't Mean a Thing If It Hasn't Got That Swing"
-and-
"I'm Not Misbehaving"
R. Chast

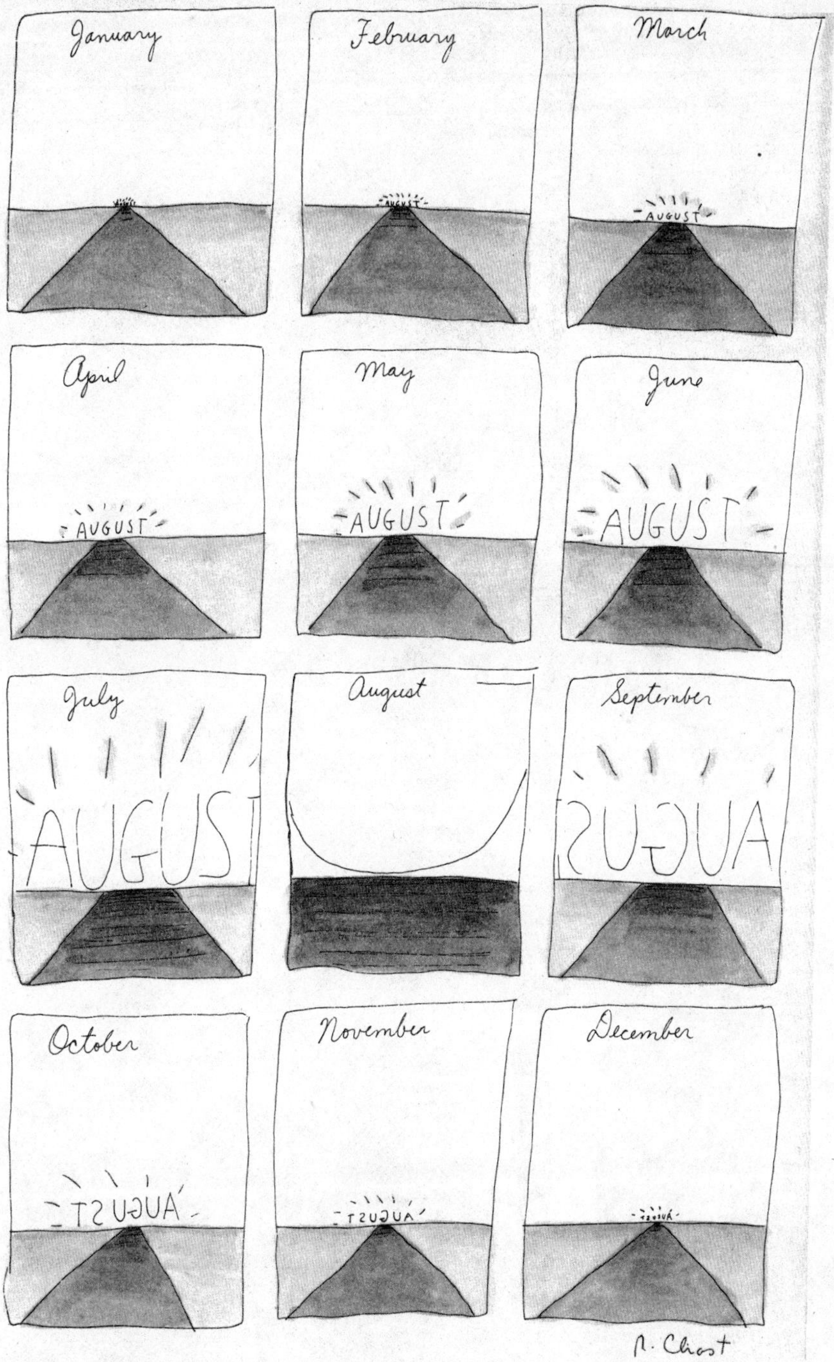
January
February
AUGUST
March
AUGUST
April
AUGUST
May
AUGUST
June
AUGUST
July
AUGUST
August
September
October
November
December
R. Chast

It's Academic

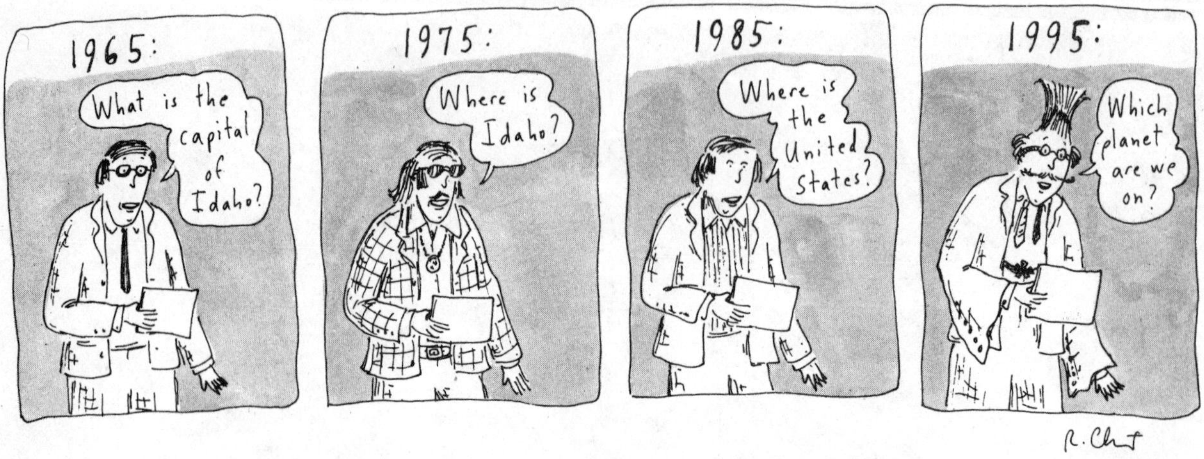
1965:
What is the capital of Idaho?
1975:
Where is Idaho?
1985:
Where is the United States?
1995:
Which planet are we on?
R. Chast

CHILDREN OF CELEBRITY CANINES

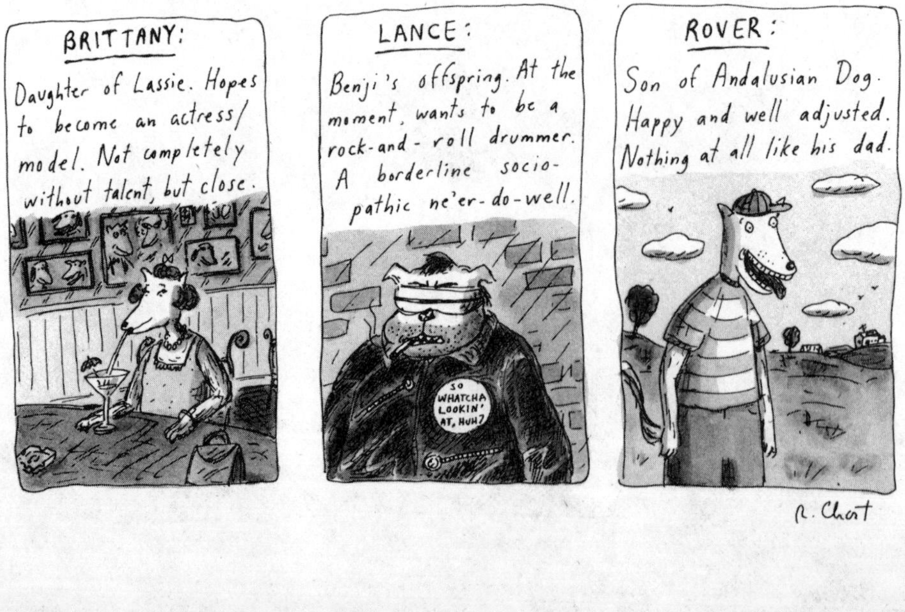
BRITTANY:
Daughter of Lassie. Hopes to become an actress/model. Not completely without talent, but close.
LANCE:
Benji's offspring. At the moment, wants to be a rock-and-roll drummer. A borderline sociopathic ne'er-do-well.
SO WHATCHA LOOKIN' AT, HUH?
ROVER:
Son of Andalusian Dog. Happy and well adjusted. Nothing at all like his dad.
R. Chast

JOURNEY TO... The Land of Enchantment

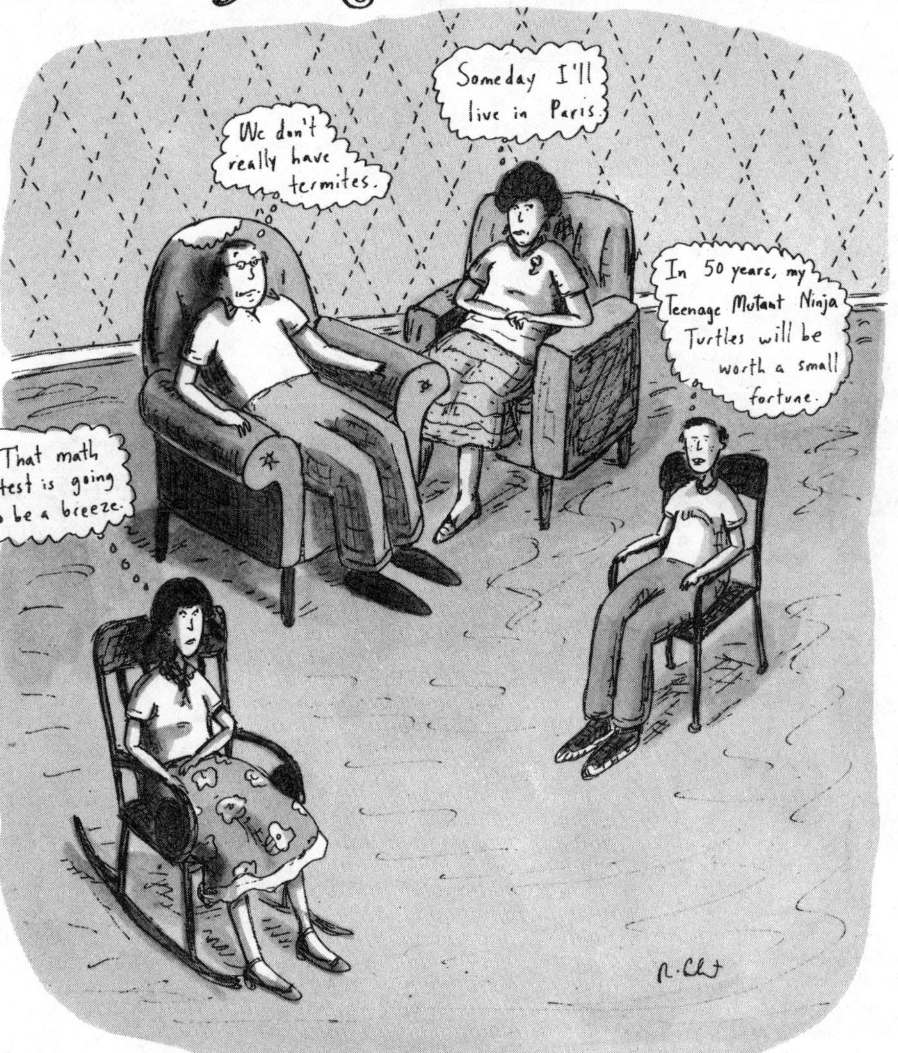

We don't really have termites.
Someday I'll live in Paris.
In 50 years, my Teenage Mutant Ninja Turtles will be worth a small fortune.
That math test is going to be a breeze.

BAR BAR

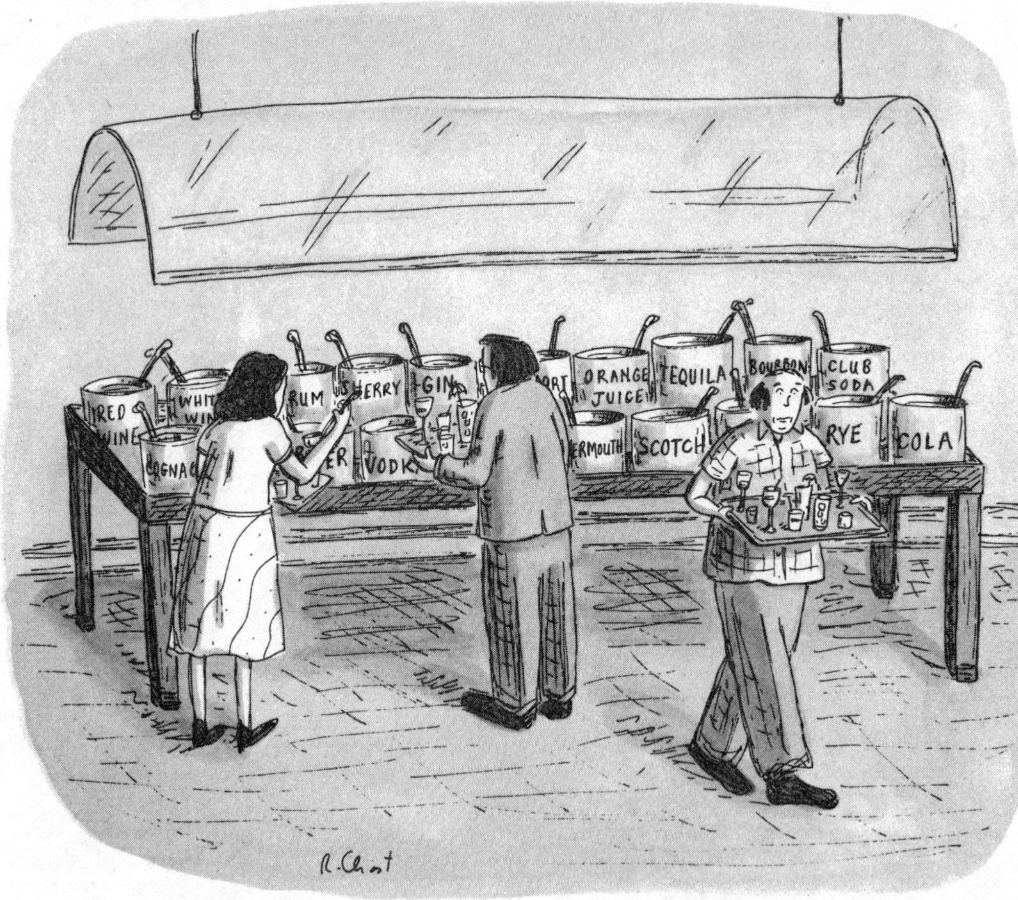
RED WINE
RUM
GIN
ORANGE JUICE
TEQUILA
BOURBON
CLUB SODA
SCOTCH
RYE
COLA
R. Chast

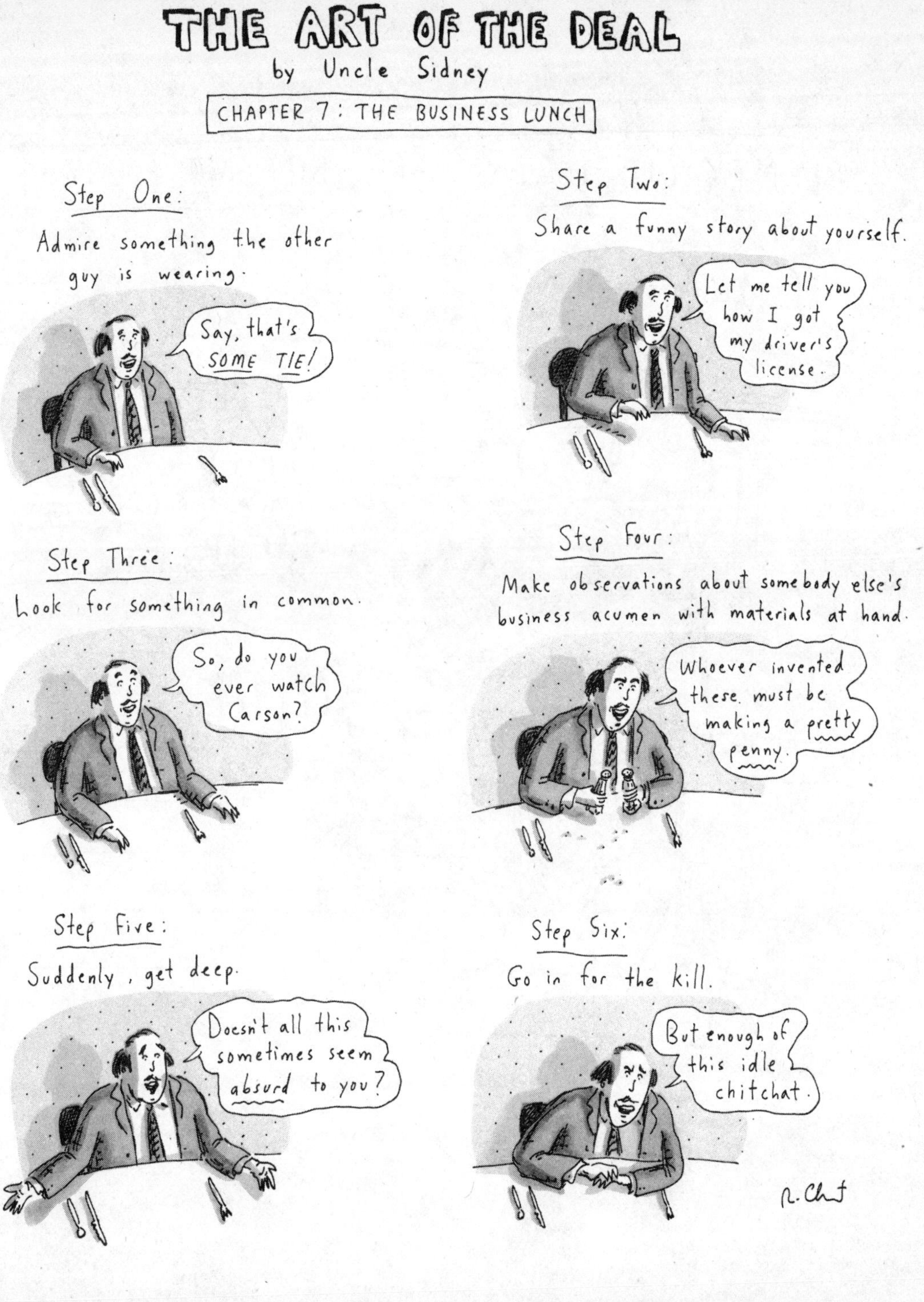
THE ART OF THE DEAL
by Uncle Sidney
CHAPTER 7: THE BUSINESS LUNCH
Step One:
Admire something the other guy is wearing.
Say, that's SOME TIE!
Step Two:
Share a funny story about yourself.
Let me tell you how I got my driver's license.
Step Three:
Look for something in common.
So, do you ever watch Carson?
Step Four:
Make observations about somebody else's business acumen with materials at hand.
Whoever invented these must be making a pretty penny.
Step Five:
Suddenly, get deep.
Doesn't all this sometimes seem absurd to you?
Step Six:
Go in for the kill.
But enough of this idle chitchat.
R. Chst

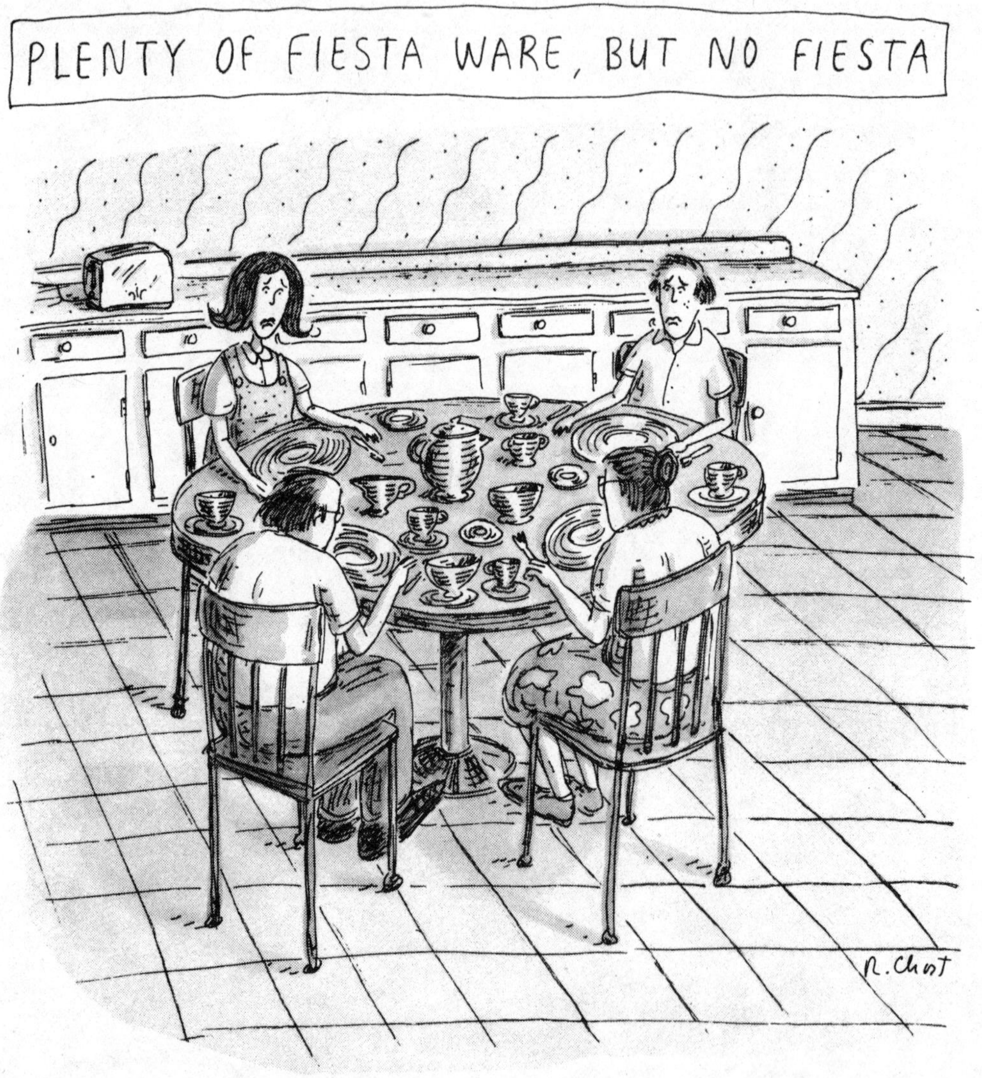
PLENTY OF FIESTA WARE, BUT NO FIESTA
R. Chast

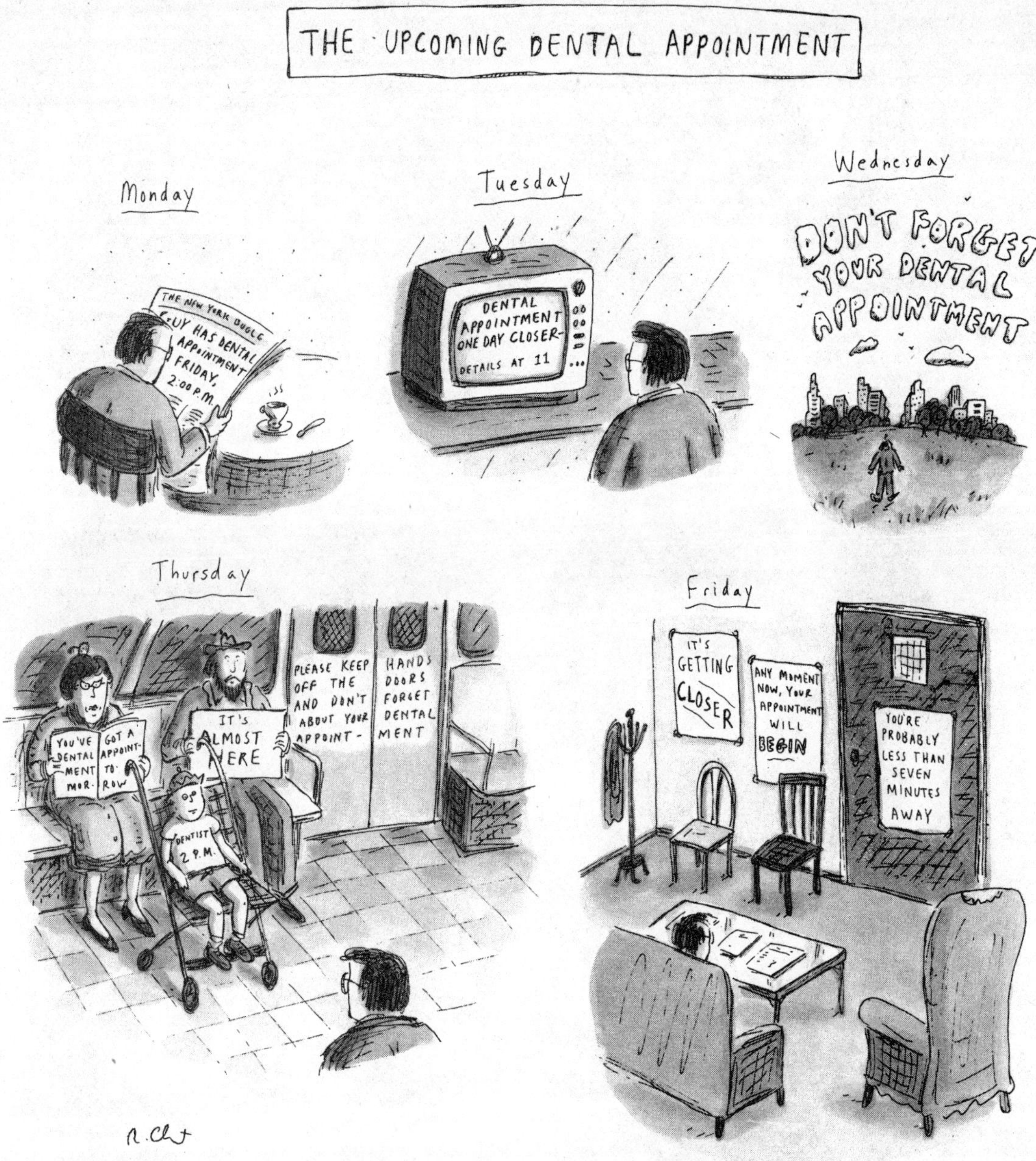
THE UPCOMING DENTAL APPOINTMENT
Monday
THE NEW YORK BUGLE
GUY HAS DENTAL APPOINTMENT FRIDAY, 2:00 P.M.
Tuesday
DENTAL APPOINTMENT ONE DAY CLOSER- DETAILS AT 11
Wednesday
DON'T FORGET YOUR DENTAL APPOINTMENT
Thursday
YOU'VE GOT A DENTAL APPOINT-MENT TO-MOR-ROW
IT'S ALMOST HERE
DENTIST 2 P.M.
PLEASE KEEP HANDS OFF THE DOORS AND DON'T FORGET ABOUT YOUR DENTAL APPOINT- MENT
Friday
IT'S GETTING CLOSER
ANY MOMENT NOW, YOUR APPOINTMENT WILL BEGIN
YOU'RE PROBABLY LESS THAN SEVEN MINUTES AWAY

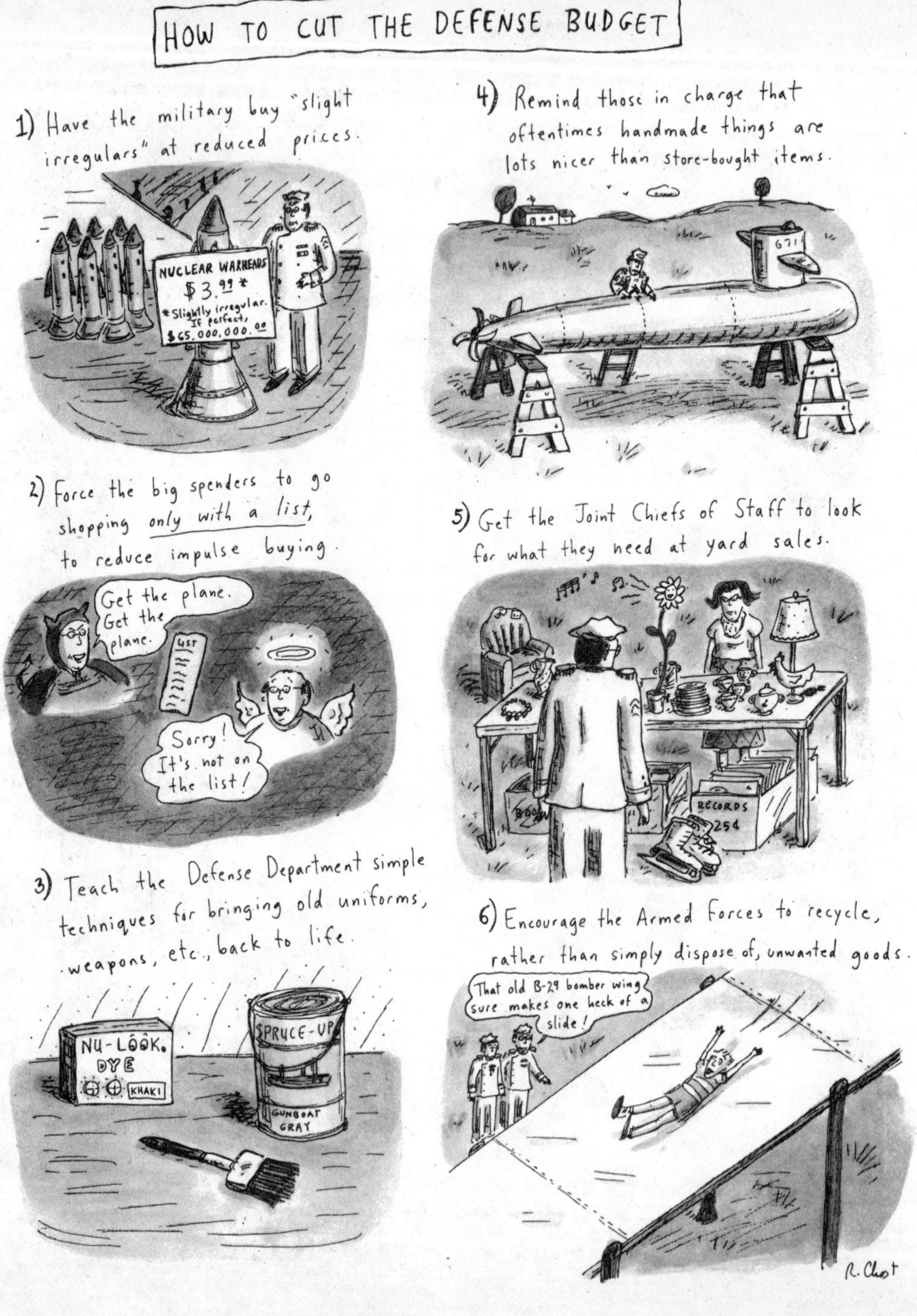
HOW TO CUT THE DEFENSE BUDGET
1) Have the military buy "slight irregulars" at reduced prices.
NUCLEAR WARHEADS $3.99* *Slightly irregular. If perfect, $65,000,000.00
2) Force the big spenders to go shopping only with a list, to reduce impulse buying.
Get the plane. Get the plane.
LIST
Sorry! It's not on the list!
3) Teach the Defense Department simple techniques for bringing old uniforms, weapons, etc., back to life.
NU-LOOK DYE KHAKI
SPRUCE-UP GUNBOAT GRAY
4) Remind those in charge that oftentimes handmade things are lots nicer than store-bought items.
671
5) Get the Joint Chiefs of Staff to look for what they need at yard sales.
RECORDS 25¢
6) Encourage the Armed Forces to recycle, rather than simply dispose of, unwanted goods.
That old B-29 bomber wing sure makes one heck of a slide!
R. Chast

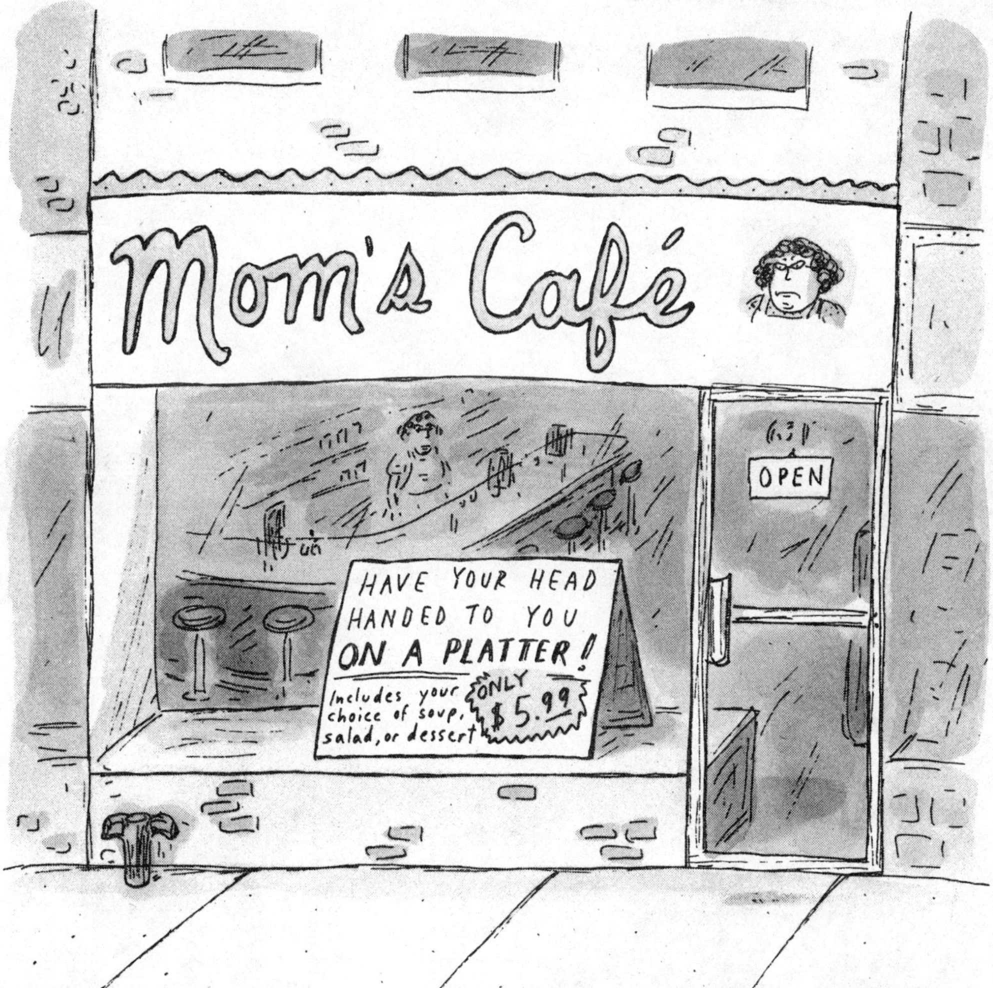
Mom's Café
OPEN
HAVE YOUR HEAD HANDED TO YOU ON A PLATTER!
Includes your choice of soup, salad, or dessert
ONLY $5.99
R. Chast

HOW TO WRITE YOUR NOVEL
① Clear your head of all distractions.
If that little bump doesn't go away by next Tuesday, I'll call Dr. Fitch.
② Concentrate on what it is you most really want to write about.
If those red dots don't go away by next Saturday, I'll call Dr. Hoskins.
③ Don't write as if there are 50 TV cameras watching your every move. Try to be uninhibited.
If that raised area doesn't go away by next Friday, I'll call Dr. Bergenson.
④ Just remember, Rome wasn't built in a day.
If that tingling sensation doesn't go away by next Monday, I'll call Dr. Pelver.
R. Chast

MARTHA STEWART
TAKES OVER THE UNIVERSE
Formal Dinner for Twenty-four on Mars
Make sure your lighting is apropos!
Sunday Brunch for Eight on Pluto
Freshly cut flowers are a must!
Ultra-Perfect Christmas Feast for Two Hundred in Alpha Centauri System
Don't forget the personalized finger bowls!

JOE SCHMOE

(A DRAMATIZATION)

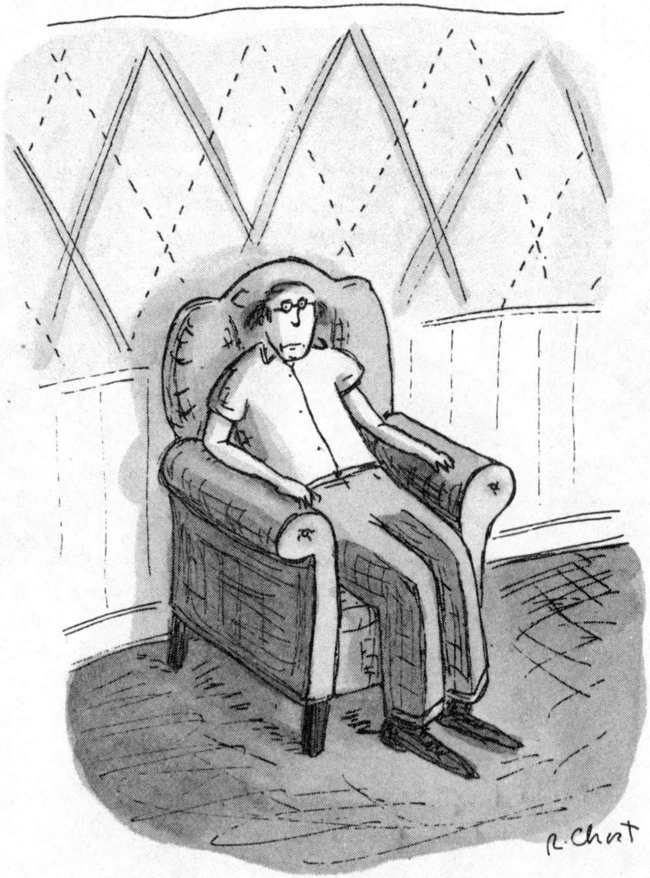
R. Chast

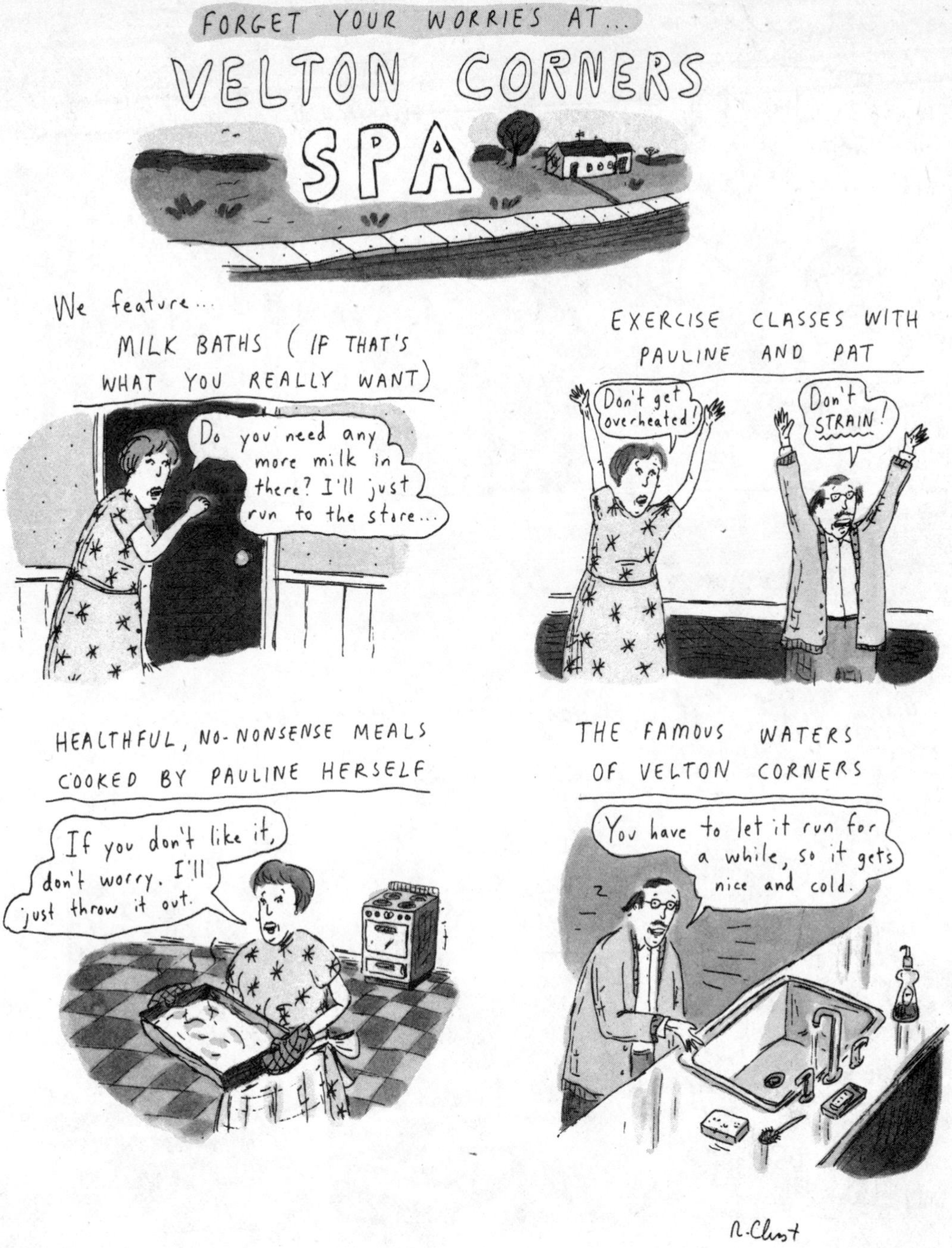
FORGET YOUR WORRIES AT...
VELTON CORNERS
SPA
We feature...
MILK BATHS (IF THAT'S WHAT YOU REALLY WANT)
Do you need any more milk in there? I'll just run to the store...
EXERCISE CLASSES WITH PAULINE AND PAT
Don't get overheated!
Don't STRAIN!
HEALTHFUL, NO-NONSENSE MEALS COOKED BY PAULINE HERSELF
If you don't like it, don't worry. I'll just throw it out.
THE FAMOUS WATERS OF VELTON CORNERS
You have to let it run for a while, so it gets nice and cold.
R. Chast

Lifetime Achievement Awards

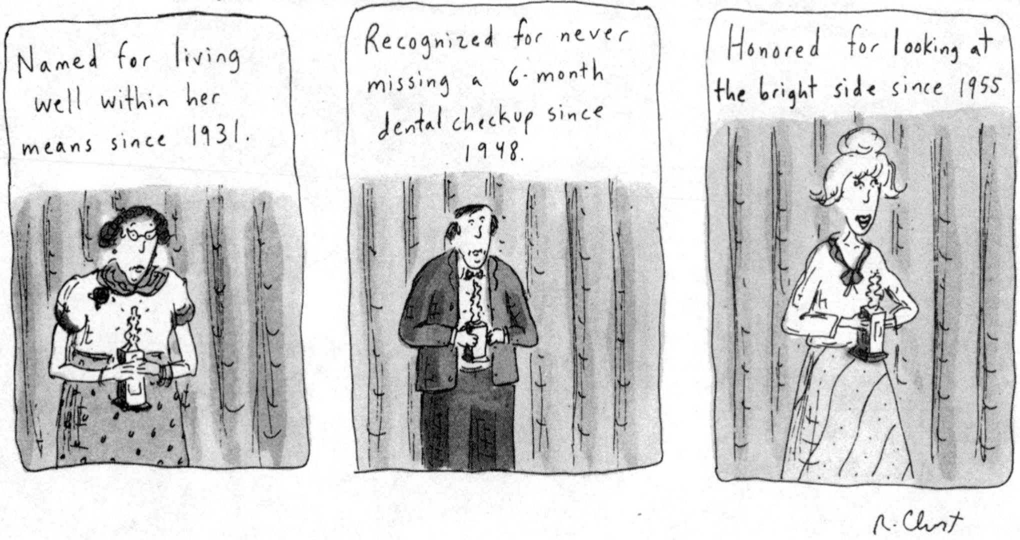
Named for living well within her means since 1931.
Recognized for never missing a 6-month dental checkup since 1948.
Honored for looking at the bright side since 1955
R. Chast

When The Cat's Away, The Mice Will...

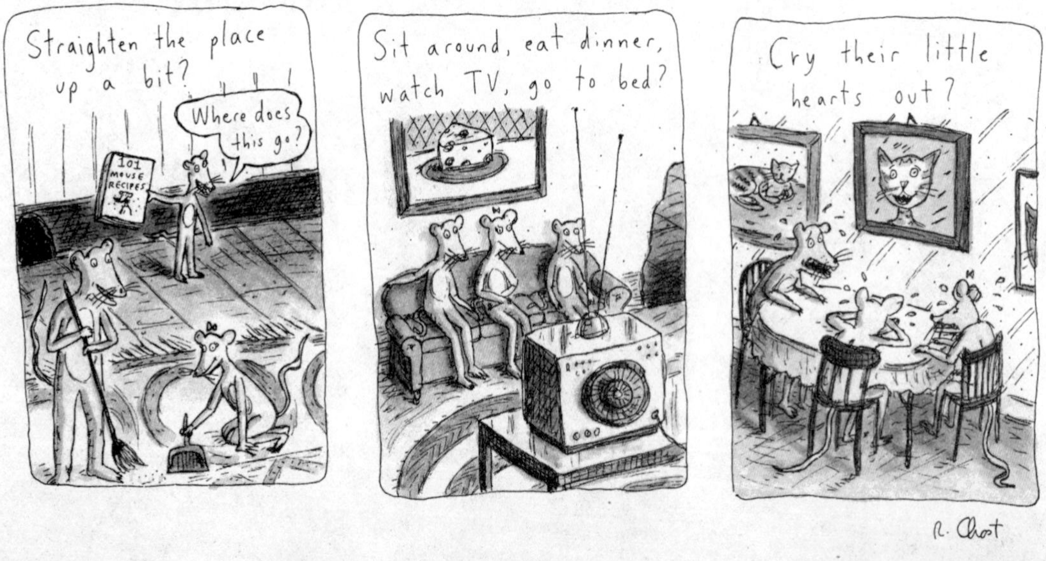
Straighten the place up a bit?
Where does this go?
101 MOUSE RECIPES
Sit around, eat dinner, watch TV, go to bed?
Cry their little hearts out?
R. Chast

RÉSUMÉ OF

CLAUDE BRISKETSON,

COMPOSER

5/18/57: "Big Bison Fight," *Natural Nature*, WNUH

11/5/63: "Cerebellum's Theme," *Your Wondrous Brain*, TV Special, WVGN

7/16/67: "The Receiver," *Phone repairman's training film*, Acme Communications

4/26/71: "Those Hilarious Owls," *Our Friends the Birds*, TV Special, WDKE

12/2/74: "Mr. Lucky in Hawaii," *The "Mr. Lucky" show*, WBEB

10/30/79: "Orange Pekoe Motif," *Promotional film*, O-So-Nice Teas, Inc.

1/14/85: "Paraguayan Segment," *South America by Bus*, Travelogues Plus Co.

R. Chast

THE WALL STREET TATTLER

★ ★ ★ ★ |(((=[]))(|4)|4|4|4 |1 3, 11 3 8 |4.   "EXCITEMENT IS OUR MIDDLE NAME"

**BIGFOOT'S
PRECIOUS METALS
INVESTMENT
STRATEGY**
                    p. 6

**ALIENS GIVE
GRANDMOTHER
STOCK MARKET
TIPS — AND NOW
SHE'S A MILLIONAIRE!**
                    p. 10

**WHAT'S YOUR
PORTFOLIO'S
HOROSCOPE?**

LIZ TAYLOR'S FINANCIAL ADVISOR BARES ALL!

"ᴍᴍ......ᴍ" ᴍᴍ ᴍᴍ

ᴍᴍᴍ ᴍᴍᴍ (ᴍᴍᴍ ᴍᴍᴍ ᴍᴍᴍ
ᴍᴍᴍ ᴍᴍᴍ ᴍᴍᴍ ᴍᴍᴍ ᴍᴍᴍ
ᴍᴍ ᴍᴍᴍ ᴍᴍᴍ ᴍᴍ ᴍᴍᴍ
ᴍᴍᴍ ᴍᴍ ᴍᴍᴍ ᴍᴍᴍ ᴍᴍ
ᴍᴍᴍ ᴍᴍ ᴍᴍᴍ ᴍᴍ

con't.p. 2

SLY AND MADONNA DISCUSS COFFEE FUTURES

LORE AND LEGEND OF THE PENNYPACKERS

How Great-Grandpa Louie Came to America with $12.00 in His Pocket and Eventually Owned a Baking Soda Factory

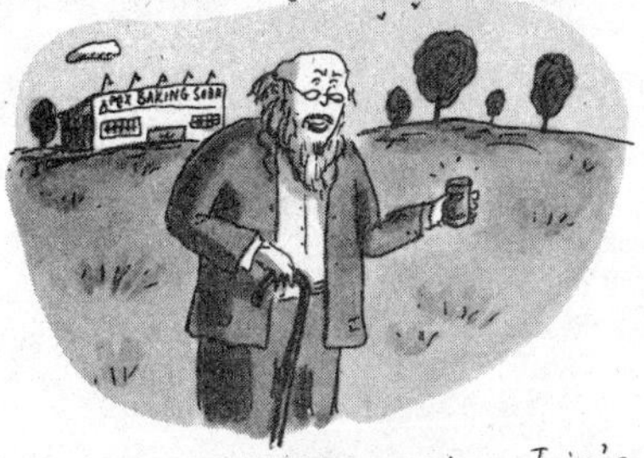
APEX BAKING SODA

The Story of Grandma Iris's Terrible Ear Infection Back in the Days Before There Was Such a Thing as Penicillin

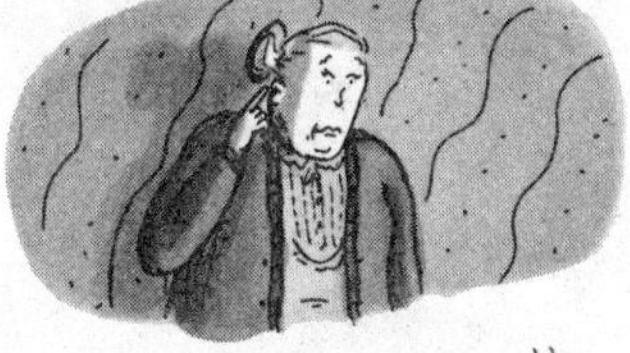

Aunt Tessie's Date with Errol Flynn's Second Cousin

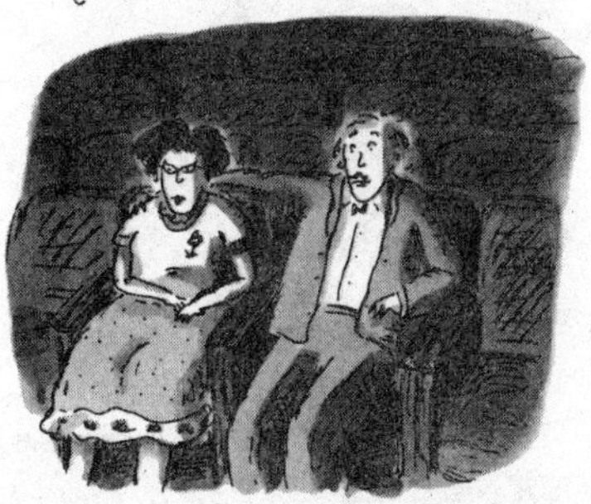

The Time the Ferris Wheel Got Stuck for an Hour and Aunt Pearl and Uncle Barney Were in the Top Car

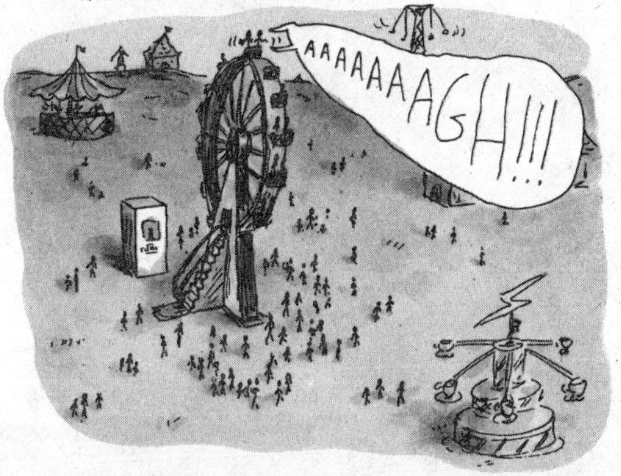
AAAAAAAGH!!!...

Cousin Gladys's Psychic Dream That Showed the Exact Location of Her Friend Doris Benson's Lost Pair of Pinking Shears

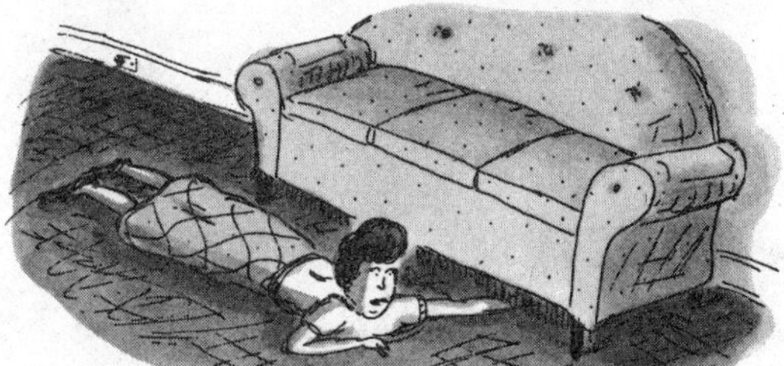

How the Connors Branch of the Family Found Itself in Hoboken, New Jersey

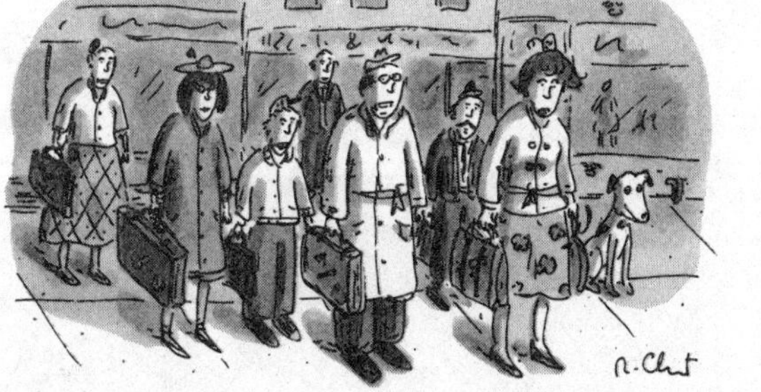
R. Chast

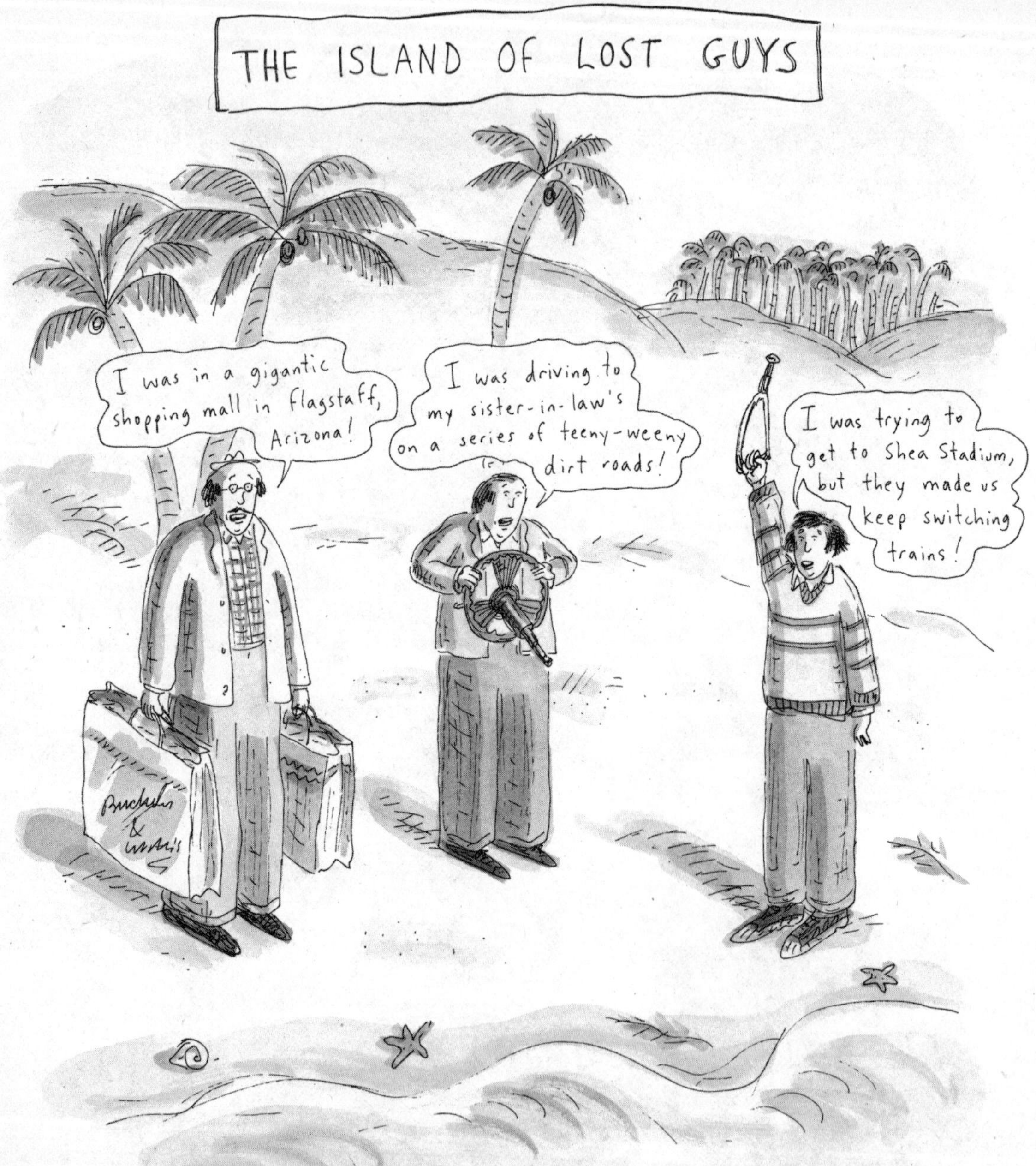
THE ISLAND OF LOST GUYS
I was in a gigantic shopping mall in Flagstaff, Arizona!
I was driving to my sister-in-law's on a series of teeny-weeny dirt roads!
I was trying to get to Shea Stadium, but they made us keep switching trains!
R. Chast

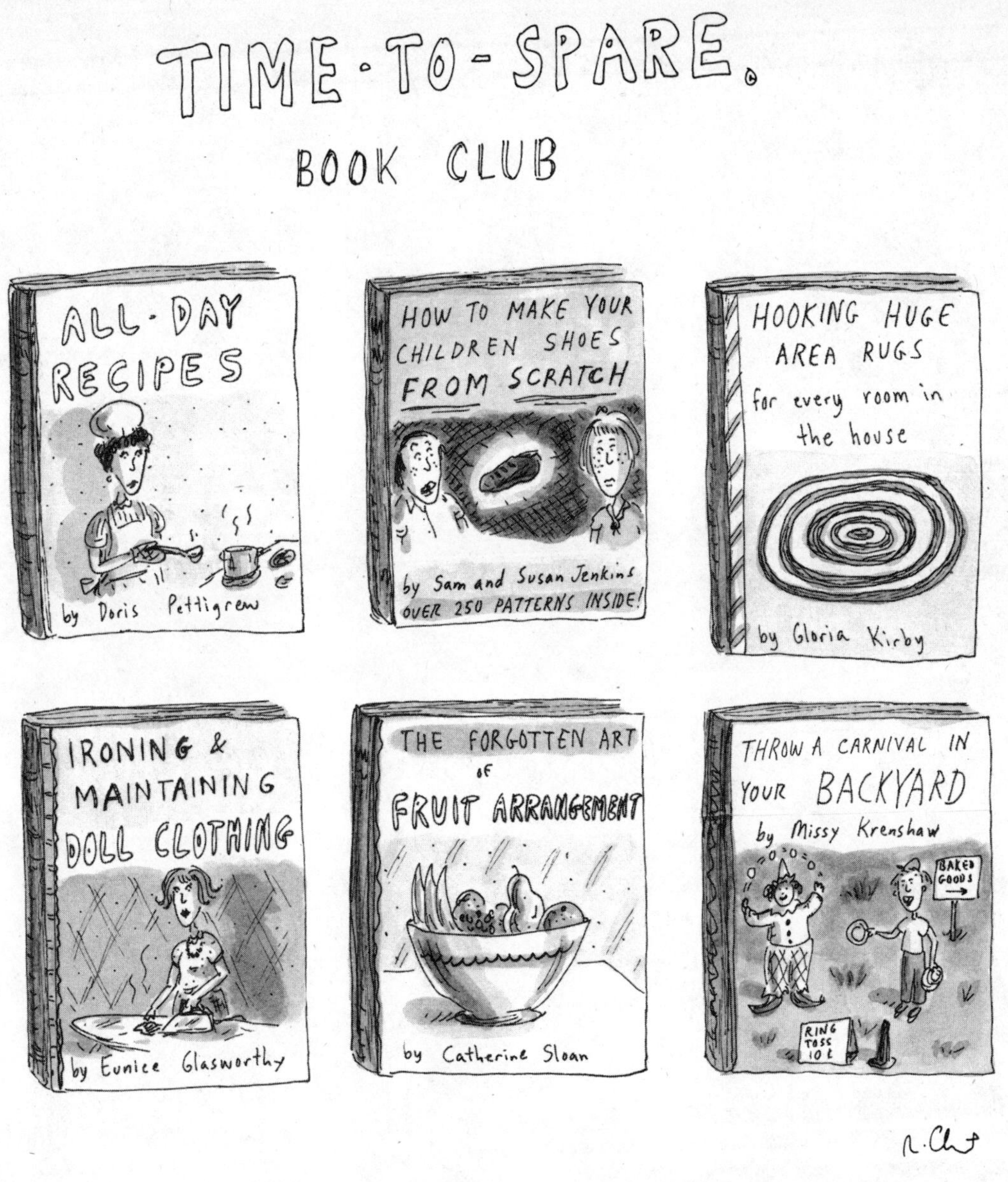
TIME-TO-SPARE.
BOOK CLUB
ALL-DAY RECIPES
by Doris Pettigrew
HOW TO MAKE YOUR CHILDREN SHOES FROM SCRATCH
by Sam and Susan Jenkins
OVER 250 PATTERNS INSIDE!
HOOKING HUGE AREA RUGS
for every room in the house
by Gloria Kirby
IRONING & MAINTAINING DOLL CLOTHING
by Eunice Glasworthy
THE FORGOTTEN ART OF FRUIT ARRANGEMENT
by Catherine Sloan
THROW A CARNIVAL IN YOUR BACKYARD
by Missy Krenshaw
BAKED GOODS
RING TOSS 10¢
R. Chast

NOT THE DEPRESSION MENTALITY

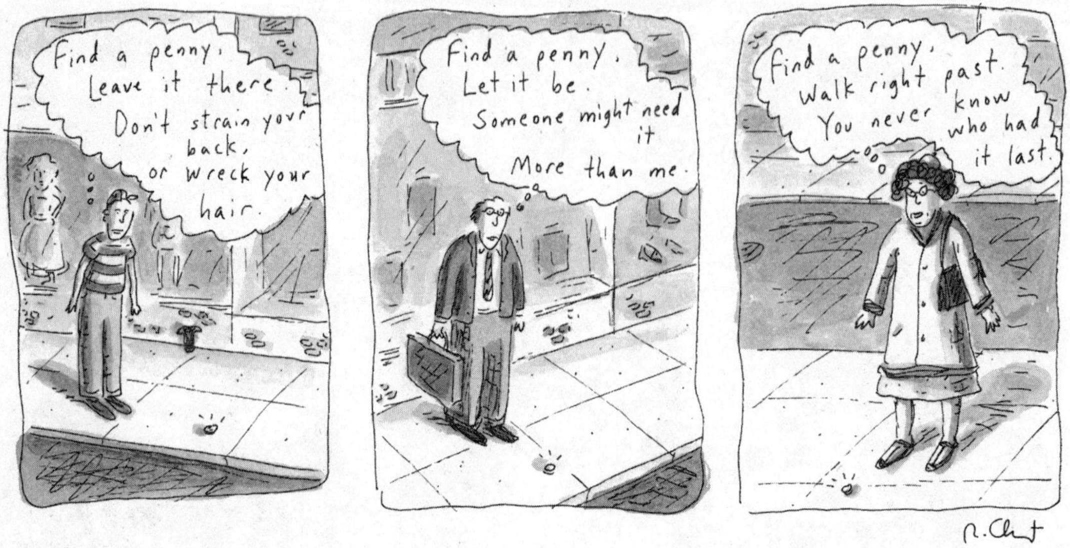
Find a penny, Leave it there. Don't strain your back, or wreck your hair.
Find a penny. Let it be. Someone might need it More than me.
Find a penny, Walk right past. You never know who had it last.

CHILDPROOFING YOUR HOME

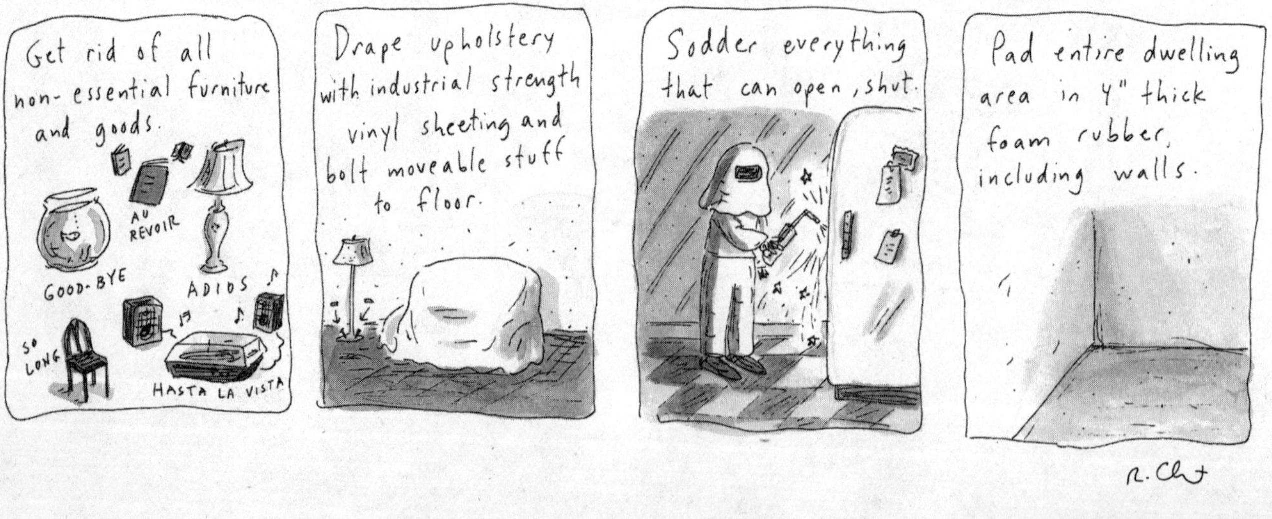
Get rid of all non-essential furniture and goods.
AU REVOIR
GOOD-BYE
ADIOS
SO LONG
HASTA LA VISTA
Drape upholstery with industrial strength vinyl sheeting and bolt moveable stuff to floor.
Sodder everything that can open, shut.
Pad entire dwelling area in 4" thick foam rubber, including walls.

JOHN B.:
BEST ENTERTAINMENT VALUE FOR UNDER $1.79

BOTTOM-OF-THE-BARREL
HOLIDAY RELEASES
The Blob vs. Rudolph
Low-budget horror-fest about malevolent protoplasm and nerdy deer.
Attack of the 2,000-Foot-Tall Santa
Santa gets exposed to radiation; enlarges; acts out.
Frosty Hangs Ten
Demented teenpic about snow-man whose dream it is to go to Hawaii and surf Pipeline.
Why is everybody being so DISCOURAGING?
R. Chast

THE SEVEN DEADLY SINS

Envy
Gee, I wish I'd ordered what he ordered.
Envy
If only he were MINE!
Envy
I wouldn't mind being disgustingly rich, no sirree Bob.
Envy
It INFURIATES me to know that there are people who are better off, smarter, and more attractive than I am.
Envy
I'm so great I'm almost jealous of myself!
Envy
Why bother moving from this sofa ~ my life will never be as good as Henry's anyway.
Envy
LIFE STYLES OF FORTUNE'S FAVORITES (i.e., NOT YOU)
R. Chast

What Children Overhear

...She bent down to pick up the pencil, and when she stood up, she was BLIND IN HER LEFT EYE.
...When he woke up, his feet had swollen to the size of WATERMELONS.
...Her scalp became infected, so they had to remove it.
...His fingernails all fell off, one by one.
...They drilled a hole in his larynx and put in a pipe that stretched CLEAR ACROSS THE ROOM.
...Mrs. Cleary's son was born with two stomachs, but he didn't find out til he was thirty-six.
R. Chast

THE LAST OF THE MOM AND POP
BROKERAGE HOUSES

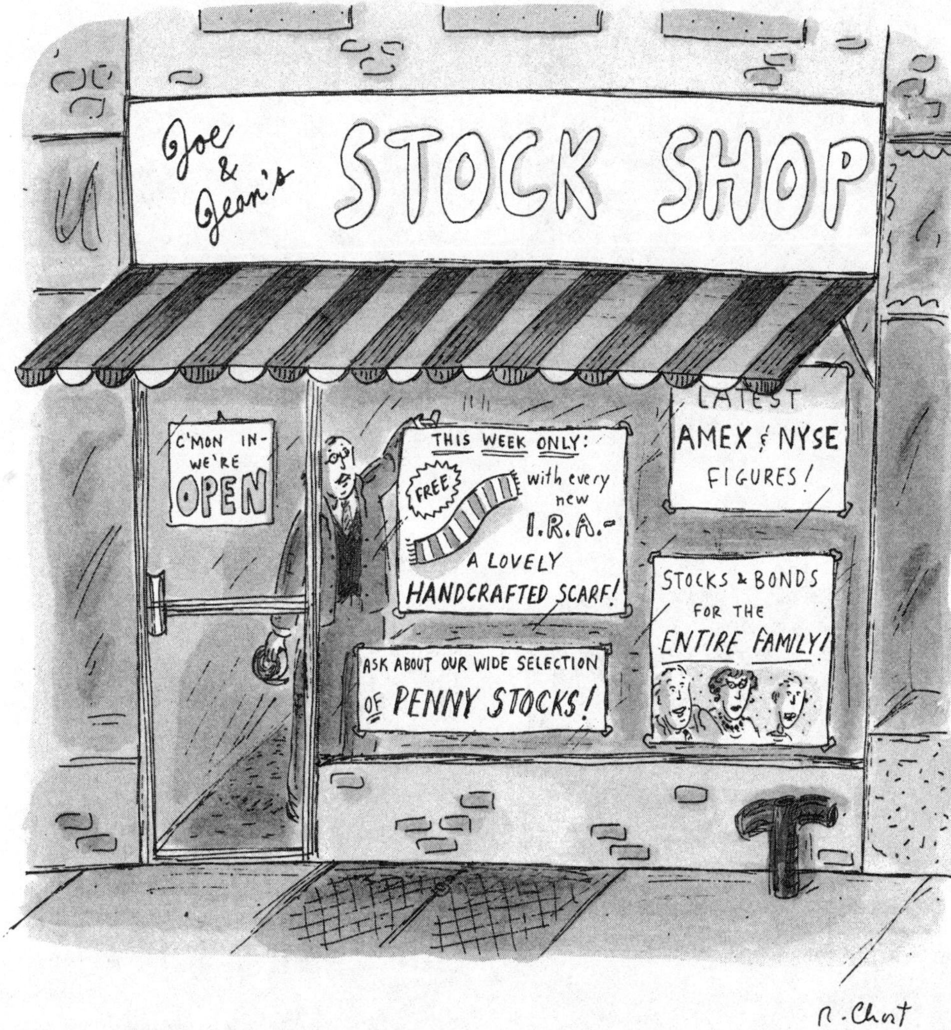
Joe & Jean's
STOCK SHOP
C'MON IN- WE'RE OPEN
THIS WEEK ONLY:
FREE
with every new I.R.A.-
A LOVELY HANDCRAFTED SCARF!
LATEST AMEX & NYSE FIGURES!
STOCKS & BONDS FOR THE ENTIRE FAMILY!
ASK ABOUT OUR WIDE SELECTION OF PENNY STOCKS!
R. Chast

THEIR PERMANENT RESIDENCES

Eric L.:
Traffic circle, Route 532

Marlene T.:
Examining table, All-
Health Clinic

Jerry K.:
Math classroom, Westview
Junior High School

Dorothy B.:
Checkout line, Food-Fare
Supermarket

RORSCHACH'S PARENTS

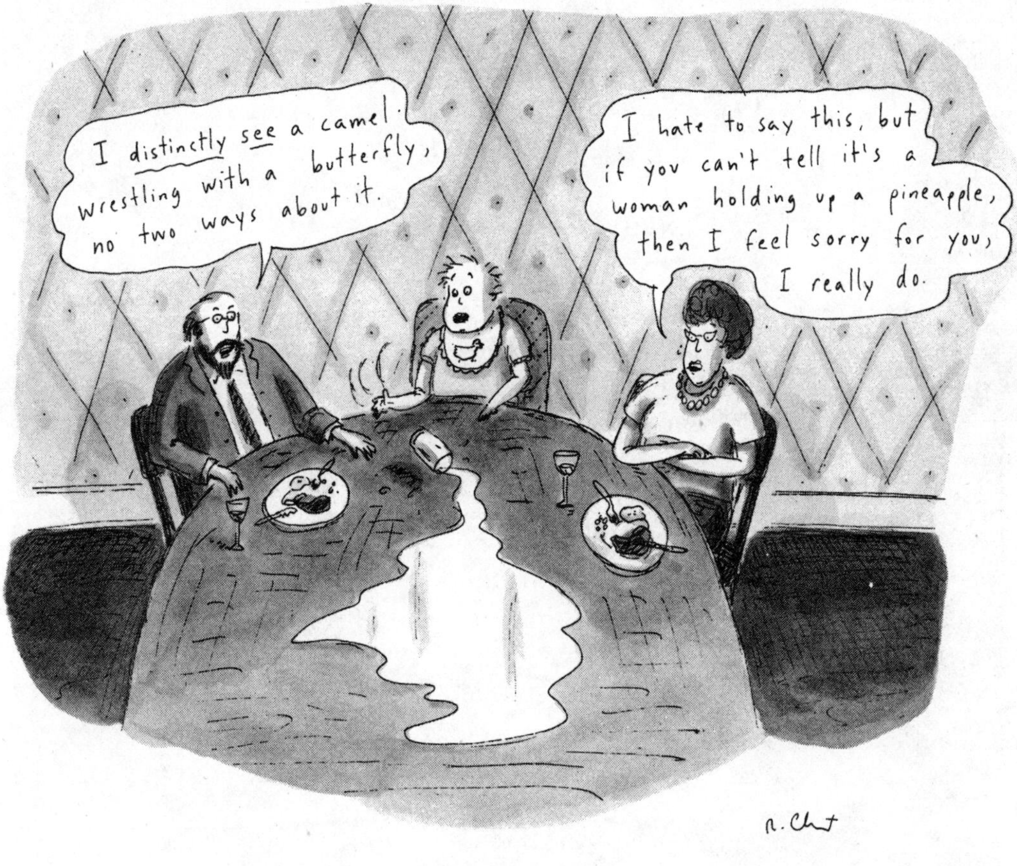
I distinctly see a camel wrestling with a butterfly, no two ways about it.
I hate to say this, but if you can't tell it's a woman holding up a pineapple, then I feel sorry for you, I really do.

LUKE WARM & OVER E-Z:

THE WORLD'S BLANDEST RAPPERS

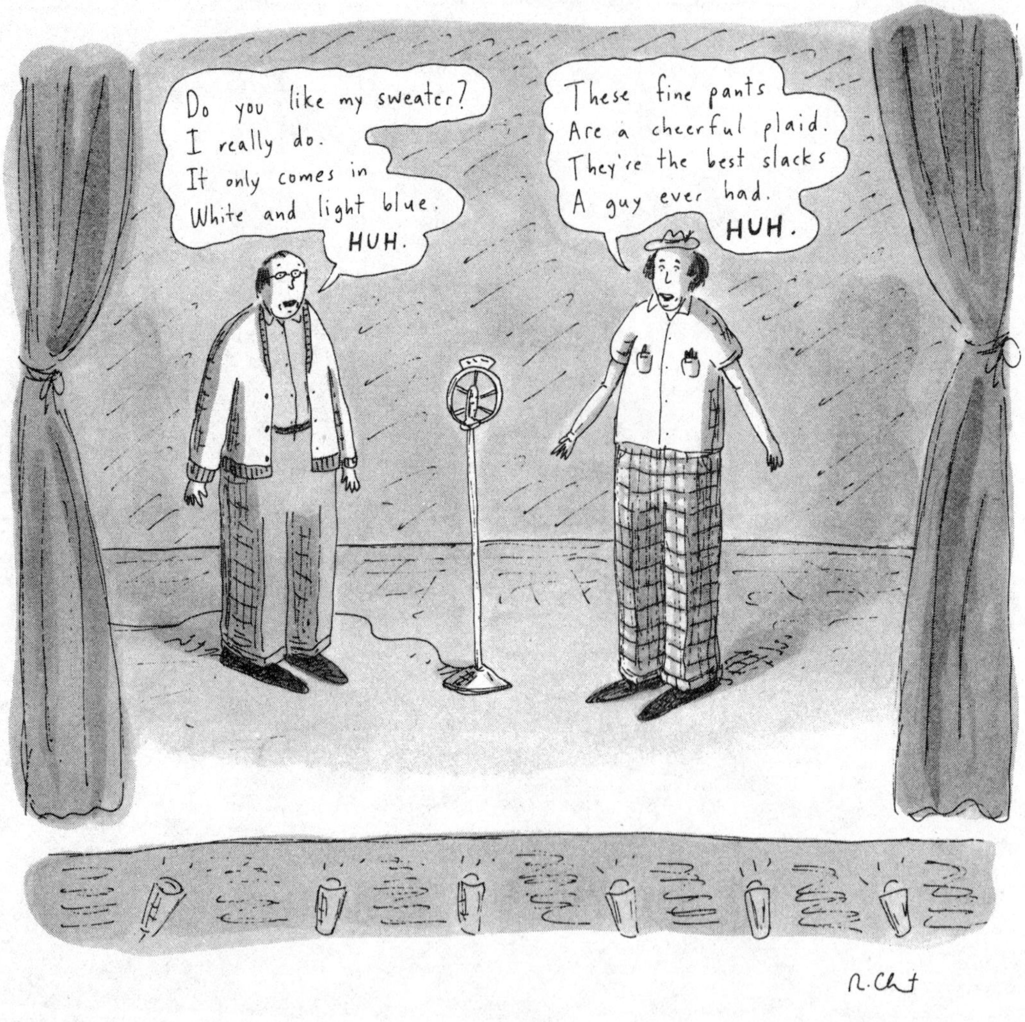
Do you like my sweater? I really do. It only comes in White and light blue. HUH.
These fine pants Are a cheerful plaid. They're the best slacks A guy ever had. HUH.
R. Cht

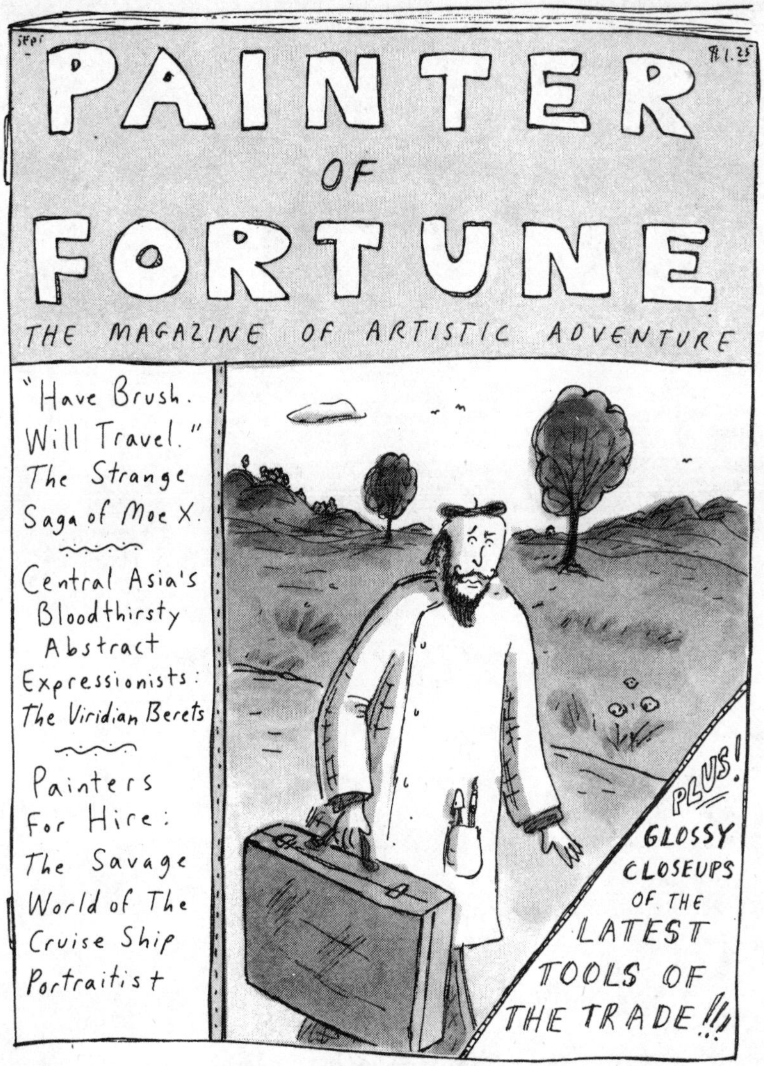
SEPT
$1.25
PAINTER OF FORTUNE
THE MAGAZINE OF ARTISTIC ADVENTURE
"Have Brush. Will Travel." The Strange Saga of Moe X.
Central Asia's Bloodthirsty Abstract Expressionists: The Viridian Berets
Painters For Hire: The Savage World of The Cruise Ship Portraitist
PLUS!
GLOSSY CLOSEUPS OF THE LATEST TOOLS OF THE TRADE!!!

R. Chast

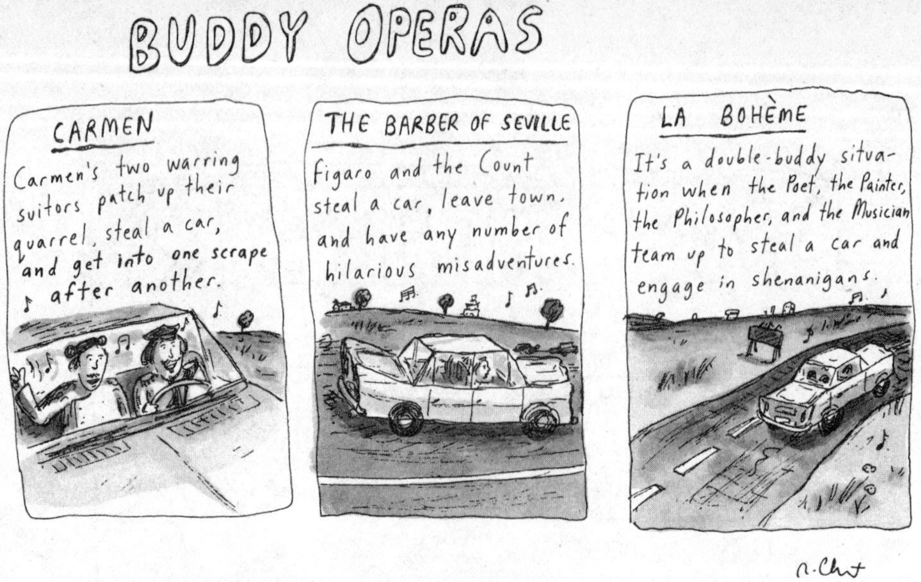
BUDDY OPERAS
CARMEN
Carmen's two warring suitors patch up their quarrel, steal a car, and get into one scrape after another.
THE BARBER OF SEVILLE
Figaro and the Count steal a car, leave town, and have any number of hilarious misadventures.
LA BOHÈME
It's a double-buddy situation when the Poet, the Painter, the Philosopher, and the Musician team up to steal a car and engage in shenanigans.

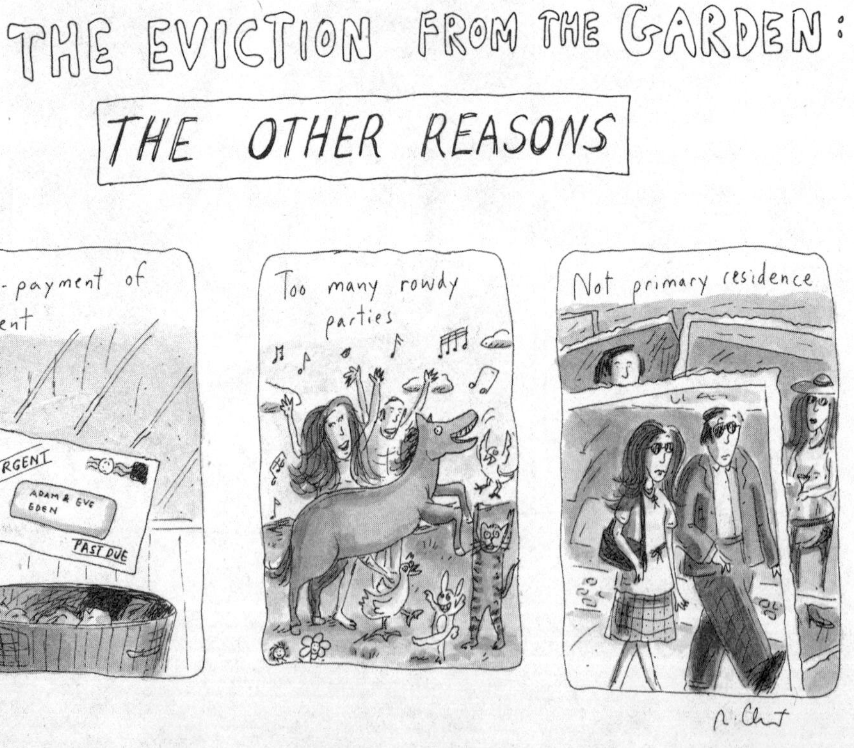
THE EVICTION FROM THE GARDEN:
THE OTHER REASONS
Non-payment of rent
URGENT
ADAM & EVE
EDEN
PAST DUE
Too many rowdy parties
Not primary residence

TIME-OFF COUPONS
10 MINUTES OFF
YOUR NEXT WAIT IN LINE
PRESENT TO THE PERSON IN FRONT OF YOU
10 MINUTES
2 MINUTES OFF
ANY CONVERSATION ANYWHERE
AT A PARTY · ON THE PHONE · ON A BUS, TRAIN, ETC.
VALID AT ANY TIME
2 MINUTES
5 MINUTES OFF
YOUR NEXT DENTAL APPOINTMENT
PRESENT AT BEGINNING OF SESSION
5 MINUTES
20 MINUTES OFF
ANY UPCOMING TRIP TO ANY AMUSEMENT PARK IN THE U.S.A.
BUST-A-GUT-LAND
EXPIRES 9/3/92
20 minutes
R. Chast

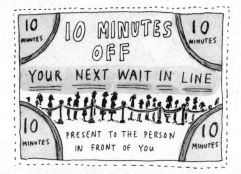

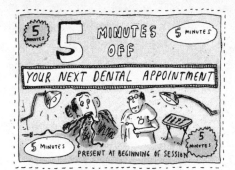

The Decoded Fashion Statements of Rhonda Perlmutter III

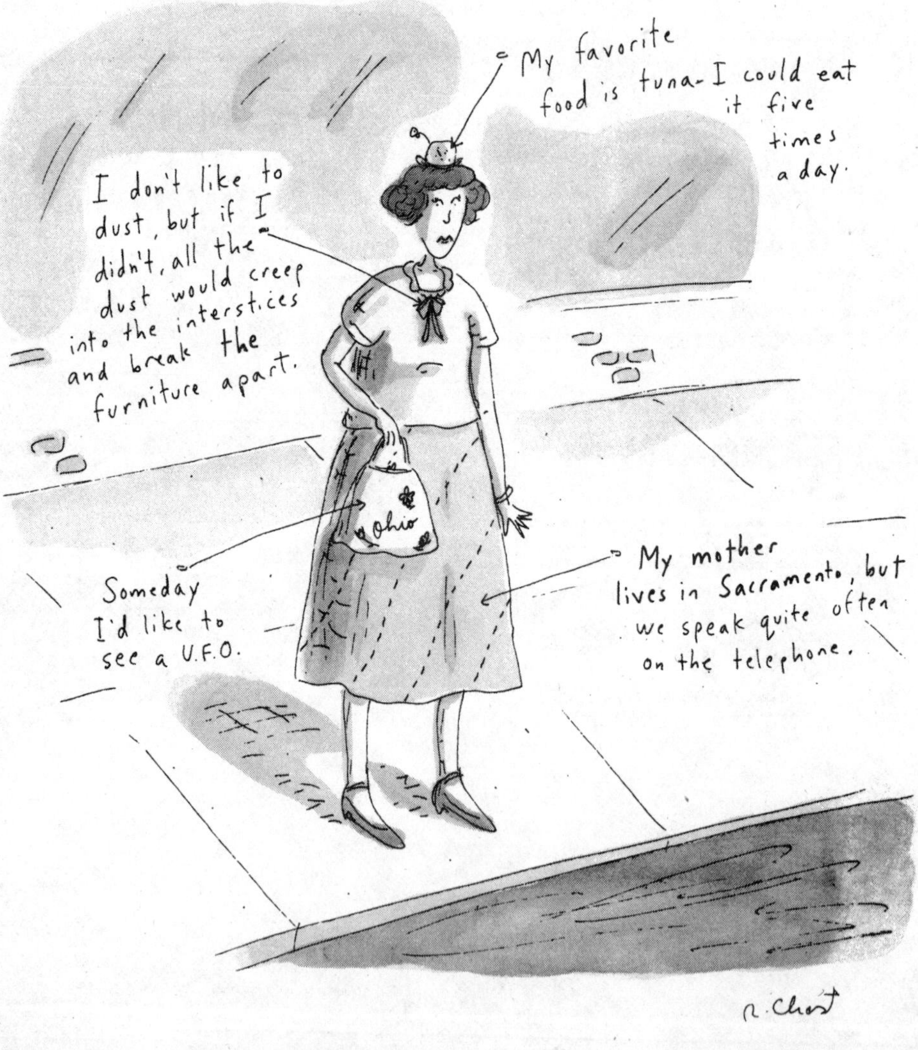

My favorite food is tuna- I could eat it five times a day.
I don't like to dust, but if I didn't, all the dust would creep into the interstices and break the furniture apart.
Ohio
Someday I'd like to see a U.F.O.
My mother lives in Sacramento, but we speak quite often on the telephone.
R. Chast

THE BEGINNING OF THE END

Broke down; bought microwave.

Surrendered; got word processor.

Gave up; purchased answering machine.

Threw in the towel; acquired VCR.

R. Chast

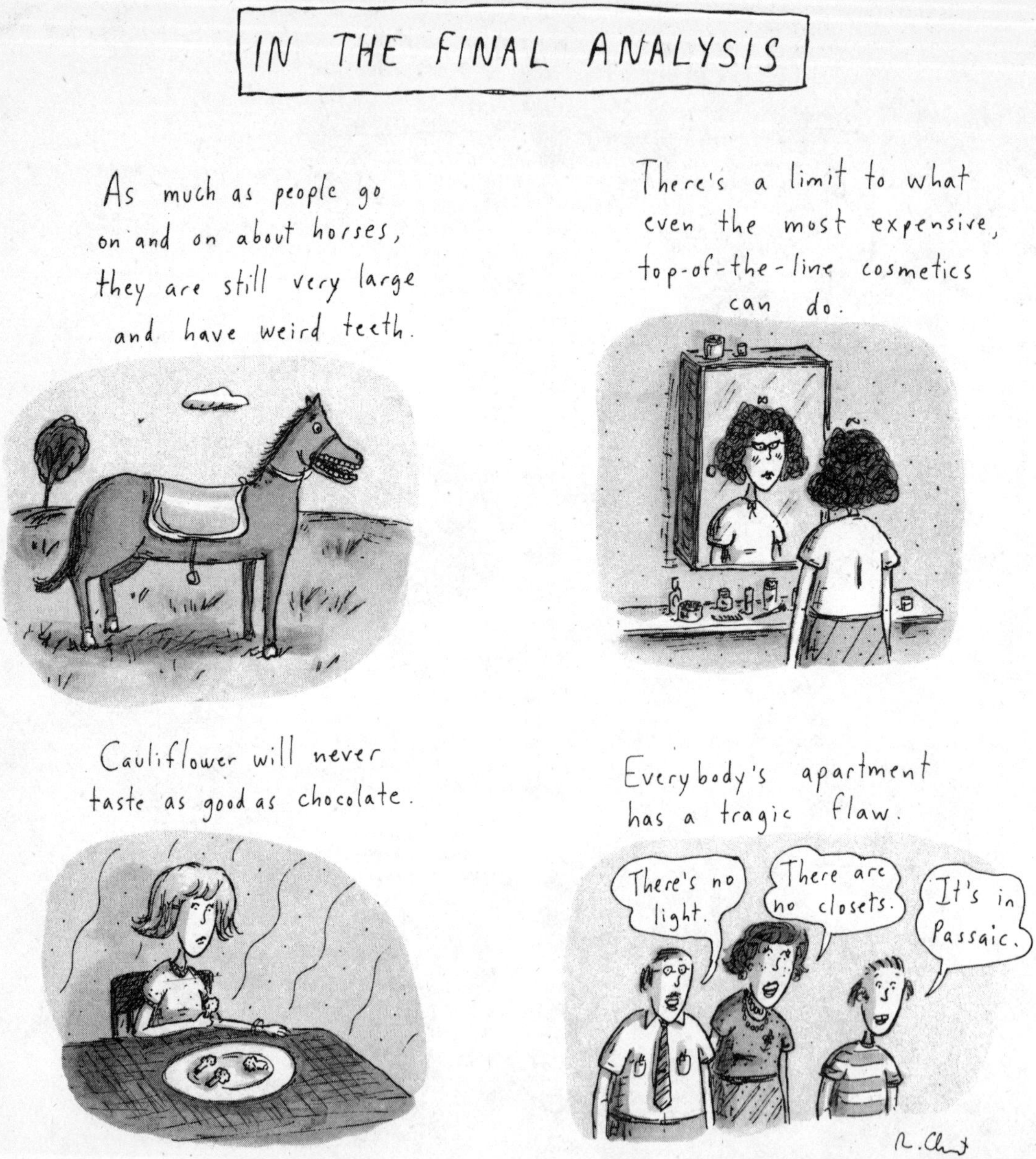
IN THE FINAL ANALYSIS
As much as people go on and on about horses, they are still very large and have weird teeth.
There's a limit to what even the most expensive, top-of-the-line cosmetics can do.
Cauliflower will never taste as good as chocolate.
Everybody's apartment has a tragic flaw.
There's no light.
There are no closets.
It's in Passaic.
R. Chast